Mariel Irvine, solicitor and principal of Mariel Irvine Solicitors, founded the firm in 2002, after some years as a partner in a large insurance litigation law firm in the City. Insurers, the police, the Prison Governors' Association, the Police Superintendents' Association and others regularly instruct her regarding assault, stress at work and harassment claims; inquests; pay, discrimination and other employment disputes; and privacy and data protection issues. She acted for an interested party in the London Bombings Inquests and more recently in the Manchester Arena Bombing Inquests.

Chambers has recommended Mariel as a leading practitioner in Police Law for a number of years. In 2018 the Parliamentary Review, an independent publication which aims to share best practice among policy makers and business leaders, invited her to contribute to their inaugural Law and Justice Review, as a best practice representative. She regularly gives presentations and seminars. It was a webinar on vicarious liability that triggered this book.

A Practical Guide to Vicarious Liability

A Practical Guide to Vicarious Liability

Mariel Irvine

Law Brief Publishing

Published 2018 by Law Brief Publishing, an imprint of Law Brief Publishing Ltd
30 The Parks
Minehead
Somerset
TA24 8BT

www.lawbriefpublishing.com

Paperback: 978-1-911035-79-4

In memory of my father,

Robert Hannay Irvine

PREFACE

Vicarious liability is an emotive issue when it concerns the imposition of liability on a blameless party, in circumstances where someone else is in the wrong. It is a flexible doctrine which depends on public policy. Since *Lister* in 2002, the law has been undergoing fundamental change. The Supreme Court has decided several cases in the last six years: *Armes, Mohamud, Cox, the Christian Brothers case*. These and other leading authorities are reviewed.

In *Dubai Aluminium Co Ltd v Salaam* [2002] UKHL 48 Lord Nicolls made reference to *the infinite range of circumstances where the issue arises. The crucial feature, or features, either producing or negativing liability vary widely from one case, or type of case to the next. Essentially the court makes an evaluative judgement in each case, having regard to all the circumstances and, importantly, having regard also to the assistance provided by previous court decisions...*

This book seeks to provide a practical guide to the evolving policy considerations which underpin this doctrine in the law of negligence, and in intentional and reliance torts. It states the law as it is on 15th October 2018.

Mariel Irvine
October 2018

CONTENTS

CHAPTER ONE
OVERVIEW

> *"To search for certainty and precision in vicarious liability is to undertake a quest for a chimaera. Many aspects of the law of torts are inherently imprecise."*
>
> –Per Lord Dyson in *Mohamud v WM Morrison Supermarkets plc* [2016] UKSC 11

There have been at least five decisions of the Supreme Court relevant to vicarious liability since 2012. A topic of importance in a minority of cases, and sometimes described as "geeky", has been forced into the spotlight.

What is vicarious liability? It is a legal principle. When applied, one party is substituted for another and held liable for that other party's wrongdoing. Sometimes the replacement party may be blameworthy or bear some "primary liability" of its own. At other times, it may have no primary liability.

It is an emotive issue when it concerns the imposition of liability on a blameless party, in circumstances where someone else is in the wrong. The applicability of the doctrine depends on public policy. A party is targeted in litigation because it has the financial means to satisfy a judgement, when the culpable party has not. In cases where the claimant rightly recovers compensation, the wrongdoer may be seen to escape Scott free.

When deciding whether the principle applies, the Supreme Court has suggested the depth of a party's pockets is not the most significant of several factors to be taken into account. In Cox v Ministry of Justice [2016] UKSC 10 Lord Reed said at paragraphs 20 - 22:-

> *It is, of course, true that where an individual is employed under a contract of employment, his employer is likely to have a deeper pocket, and can in any event be expected to have insured against vicarious liability. Neither of these, however, is a principled justification for imposing vicarious liability. The mere possession of wealth is not in itself any ground for imposing liability. As for insurance, employers insure themselves because they are liable: they are not liable because they have insured themselves. On the other hand, given the infinite variety of circumstances in which the question of vicarious liability might arise, it cannot be ruled out that there might be circumstances in which the absence or unavailability of insurance, or other means of meeting a potential liability, might be a relevant consideration.*

Insurers remain unconvinced. Some believe the Market is being required to fund a system of no-fault compensation. On the one hand it is right that meritorious claimants recover compensation where they have suffered damage as a result of another's wrong doing. On the other hand, there are many circumstances where insurers have indemnified policy holders who are blame free. Liability policy wordings have been reviewed following the imposition of vicarious liability for the commission of serious criminal offences. What can an organisation do to reduce the risk of engaging a future criminal who has no previous criminal convictions? Very little.

It is important to remember that the principle of vicarious liability is not confined to the law of tort. *The rationale underlying the principle holds good for equitable wrongs. The rationale also holds good for a wrong comprising a breach of a statutory duty or prohibition which gives rise to civil liability, provided always the statute does not expressly or impliedly indicate otherwise.* (Per Lord Nicholls of Bikenhead when giving judgement in *Majrowski v Guy's and St Thomas's NHS Trust [2006 UK HL 34, at paragraph 10]*

Lord Nichols went on to make a finding of vicarious liability against an NHS Trust under the Protection from Harassment Act 1997. In late 2017, in the first date leak class action, the High Court held an employer was vicariously liable for personal data breaches and criminal offences committed by an employee under the now obsolete Data Protection Act 1998: see *Various Claimants v William Morrisons Supermarket PLC* [2017] EWHC 3113. In October 2018 the Court of Appeal upheld the decision. In due course, vicarious liability may similarly be imposed under the Data Protection Act 2018.

A statute may expressly impose vicarious liability for wrongdoing. Under section 88 of the Police Act 1996, a Chief Constable may be liable "*in respect of any unlawful conduct of his servants in the course of their employment.*" The Equality Act 2010 imposes vicarious liability on employers in a range of circumstances.

Express statutory vicarious liability is not restricted to the employer/employee relationship. In *Unite the Union v Nailard* [2018] EWCA Civ 1203, the Court of Appeal held the Union was vicariously liable for the harassment perpetrated by an elected official since the official was its agent within the meaning of section 109 (2) Equality Act 2010. In an older case, the partners of a firm of solicitors were found vicariously liable for the "wrongful assistance" provided by a dishonest partner in *Dubai Aluminium Co Ltd v Salaam* [2002] UKHL 48. The partner was held to be acting in the ordinary course of the business of the firm, within the meaning of section 10 Partnership Act 1890.

The principle extends to unincorporated associations and the relationship of principle and agent at common law. In the very recent case of *Frederick v Positive Solutions (Financial Services) Limited* [2018] EWCA Civ 431, His Honour Judge Dight, sitting as a Deputy High Court judge, concluded it was not necessary to go back beyond two personal injury cases, the *Christian Brothers case* and also *Cox*, to determine the law of vicarious liability in a case of pure economic loss. The Court of Appeal upheld his decision, although it declined to consider whether any unitary modern law of vicarious liability was to be applied in a case of agency.

This book reviews the law of vicarious liability so as to provide a clear practical guide on how the principle may be applied to cases of tortious wrongdoing. In *Dubai Aluminium*, Lord Nicholls made reference to *the infinite range of circumstances where the issue arises. The crucial feature or features, either producing or negativing vicarious liability vary widely from one case, or type of case to the next. Essentially the court makes an evaluative judgement in each case, having regard to all the circumstances and, importantly, having regard also to the assistance provided by previous court decisions…*

CHAPTER TWO
NEGLIGENCE AND INTENTIONAL TORTS – STAGE ONE OF THE TWO STAGE TEST

In *E v English Province of Our Lady of Charity and another* [2012] EWCA Civ 938 Lord Tomlinson referred to:

> *...the notorious difficulty of this area of the law...*

INTRODUCTION

The general rule used to be that employers were vicariously liable for the acts and omissions of their employees in the course of their employment. They were not vicariously liable for the wrongdoing of independent contractors. It was a critical distinction for which there was (and still is where the wrongdoer is clearly an employee) a two-stage test:

1. Is the wrongdoer an employee? If so,

2. Was the wrongdoing carried out in the course of employment?

Over the past ten to fifteen years, the two-stage test has evolved so as to apply the principle of vicarious liability to relationships other than that of an employer and employee. In some circumstances, where the relationship is akin to employment, an employer may now be liable for the wrongdoing of independent contractors.

This chapter traces the development of the first stage of the test.

IS THE WRONGDOER AN EMPLOYEE?

Whether the wrongdoer is an employee is likely to be a question of mixed law and fact. As Lord Nicholls explained in *Dubai Aluminium Company Limited v Salaam* [2002] UKHL 48, deciding the question entails making a value judgement on the facts.

A written contract of employment or "*contract for service*" (as opposed to "*contract for services*") which expresses the intention of the parties in clear terms may not be conclusive. The court will look at the relationship as a whole and may come to the conclusion that the expressed intention that the wrongdoer is self-employed is simply a device to gain tax and national insurance advantages: *Ferguson v Dawson and Partners (Contractors) Limited* [1976] 1 W.L.R. 1213, a construction case.

The relationship is be examined in the round, adopting a holistic approach. The factors listed below should be taken into account: see the judgement of the Privy Council in *Lee Ting Sang v Chung Chi-Keung* [1990] 2 AC 374. It is not an exhaustive list and none of the factors is conclusive on its own. They will be given different weight depending on the surrounding circumstances.

- Does the employer control not only what work is carried out but also how the work is carried out? (But see Rix LJ's reasoning in *Viasystems* below.)

- Is the individual closely supervised?

- Is the individual an integral part of the employer's business or organisation?

- Does the individual provide his own equipment?
- Does the individual bear any financial risk as a result of the working relationship?
- Does the individual hire his own workers?
- Will the individual profit from his own good management of the work?
- Can the individual determine his own hours of work or does the employer control his working time?
- Does the individual work for the employer as his master or boss or is he in business on his own account?

In an industrial injuries case some time ago, where the issue was whether a road traffic accident occurred in the course of the driver's employment, the Court of Appeal had this to say:

> *We cannot overemphasise the importance of looking at the factual picture as a whole and rejecting any approach based on the fallacious concept that any one factor is conclusive. The addition or subtraction of one factor in a given situation may well tip the balance. In another, the addition or subtraction of the same factor may well make no difference....*
>
> – Sir John Donaldson MR in *Nancollas v Insurance Officer* [1985] I All ER 833

DUAL VICARIOUS LIABILITY

Surprisingly, two organisations may be vicariously liable for the same worker's negligence. This means that vicarious liability may attach even when the wrongdoer is not an employee. *Viasystems (Tyneside) Ltd v Thermal Transfer (Northern) Limited* [2005] EWCA Civ 1151 concerned a fitter who had caused a flood at a factory. He had been supplied on a labour only basis by the third defendant to the second defendant, and was working under the supervision of another fitter supplied on the same basis by the third defendant. Both fitters were under the supervision of a foreman contracted to the second defendant. Since both the second defendant and the third defendant were entitled to give orders as to how the work was to be done, and either could have prevented the negligent act, both were vicariously liable on the facts of this case. It did not matter that the wrongdoer's employment had not transferred from the third defendant to the second defendant. The second defendant was still liable.

Lord Justice May held:

> *To look for a transfer of a contract of employment is, in a case such as this, no more than a distracting device; in the present case a misleading one. [The fitter's mate's] employment was not transferred. The inquiry should concentrate on the relevant negligent act and then ask whose responsibility it was to prevent it. Who was entitled, and perhaps theoretically obliged, to give orders as to how the work should or should not be done?...*
>
> *If, on the facts of a particular case, the core question is who was entitled, and in theory obliged, to control the employee's relevant*

> *negligent act so as to prevent it, there will be some cases in which the sensible answer would be each of two "employers". The present is such a case.*

May LJ's test of control was the same as was applied in *Mersey Docks and Harbour Board v Coggins & Griffith* (Liverpool) Ltd [1947] AC 1.

In an interesting passage addressing the relative contributions of the second and third defendant, Lord Justice May confirmed where two parties have the necessary control, but are not themselves at fault, damages are likely to be apportioned equally.

> *For dual vicarious liability, equal contribution may, depending on the facts, be close to a logical necessity. This is because vicarious liability is a policy device of the law to redistribute the incidence of loss from a supposedly impecunious employee, who is personally at fault, to one or more supposedly solvent and insured employers, who are not personally at fault. The court is not, therefore, concerned to look for personal responsibility in the employer based on what might otherwise have been direct responsibility.... Vicarious liability derives from the relationship between the employee and the employers, the critical relationship being the employer's right (and theoretical obligation) to control the relevant activity of the employee. If the relationships yield dual control, it is highly likely at least that the measure of control will be equal, for otherwise the court would be unlikely to find dual control.*

Lord Justice Rix provided his own reasons for reaching the same decision on vicarious liability [emphasis added]:

> *In my judgement, if consideration is given to the function and purposes of the doctrine of vicarious liability, then the possibility of dual responsibility provides a coherent solution to the problem of the borrowed employee..... However, I am a little sceptical that the doctrine of dual vicarious liability is to be wholly equated with the question of control...I would hazard... the view that what one is looking for is a situation where the employee in question, at any rate for relevant purposes,* ***is so much a part of the work, business or organisation of both employers that it is just to make both employers answer for his negligence.*** *What has to be recalled is that the vicarious liability in question is one which involves no fault on the part of the employer. It is a doctrine designed for the sake of the claimant imposing a liability incurred without fault because the employer is treated by the law as picking up the burden of an organisational or business relationship which he has undertaken for his own benefit.*

It is clear that an employer can be vicariously liable for the employee of an independent contractor, contrary to the old general rule, so long as it exercises a sufficient degree of control over that employee. An employer may also be liable where an employee is so much a part of the work, business or organisation of both employers that it is fair, just and convenient for both to bear the risk of the employee's negligence.

IS THE RELATIONSHIP "AKIN" TO EMPLOYMENT?

The doctrine has been extended, so that where the relationship is "akin to employment", vicarious liability may be established. There is no need to create the legal fiction that the wrongdoer is in fact employed.

In *E v English Province of Our Lady of Charity and another* [2012] EWCA Civ 938 the judge at first instance had to decide, as a preliminary issue, whether a bishop might be vicariously liable for sexual assaults committed by a priest in his diocese. MacDuff J, gave a helpful review of the development of the law.

> *....Until recent years the courts concentrated on employment as underpinning vicarious liability. Where that relationship was in doubt the court would look at all the circumstances and treat the relationship as one of employment where certain criteria, not always easy to discern in abstract, were met. The court would look at the nature of the relationship where the third party workman was supplied by some other party (an independent contractor) or where he was said to be self-employed. In Short v J&W Henderson Ltd (1946) 62 TLR 427 employment was determined by the application of the "control test". Where a component of the relationship was one of control of the manner of the work the relationship was deemed to be one of employment.*

In the *E*, the second defendant conceded on behalf of the bishop that vicarious liability can be founded on a relationship other than employment. In what Lord Phillips later described in the

Christian Brothers case as a *lucid and bold judgement* MacDuff J found that the relationship between the wrongdoer and the bishop was *akin to employment* and vicarious liability could attach.

The second defendant appealed on this issue and the Court of Appeal had to review whether the bishop could be vicariously liable. Lord Justice Ward distilled the essence of being an employee down to *he is paid a wage or salary to work under some, even if only slight, control of his employer in his employer's business for that business. Father Baldwin may not quite match every facet of being an employee but in my judgement he is very close to it indeed... Father Baldwin is more like an employee than an independent contractor. He is in a relationship with his bishop which is close enough and so akin to employer/employee as to make it just and fair to impose vicarious liability. Justice and fairness is used here as a salutary check on the conclusion. It is not a standalone test for a conclusion.*

SYNTHESIS OF THE TWO STAGE TEST

In *Various Claimants v Catholic Child Welfare Society* (*the Christian Brothers case*) [2010] EWCA Civ 1106 Hughes LJ laid emphasis upon the fact –sensitive nature of the two stage inquiry which it is necessary to undertake when examining whether A is vicariously responsible for the acts of B and concluded, that "*it is a judgement upon the synthesis of the two stages which is required.*"

When the case reached the Supreme Court, Lord Phillips clarified this synthesis as meaning:

1. Consideration of the relationship of D1 and D2 to see whether it is one that is capable of giving rise to vicarious liability;

2. Consideration of the connection that links the relationship between D1 and D2 with the act or omission of D1.

He also listed, at paragraph 35 of his judgement, the various criteria which makes it fair, just and reasonable to impose vicarious liability on employers for their employees:

1. *The employer is more likely to have the means to compensate the victim than the employee and can be expected to have insured against that liability;*

2. *The tort will have been committed as a result of activity being taken by the employee on behalf of the employer;*

3. *The employee's activity is likely to be part of the business activity of the employer;*

4. *The employer, by employing the employee to carry on the activity will have created the risk of the tort committed by the employee;*

5. *The employee will, to a greater or lesser degree, have been under the control of the employer*

At paragraph 47 Lord Phillips went on:

At paragraph 35 above I have identified those incidents of the relationship between employer and employee that it make it fair, just and reasonable to impose vicarious liability on a defendant. Where the defendant and tortfeasor are not bound by a contract of employment, but their relationship has the same incidents, that relationship can properly give rise to vicarious liability on the ground that it is "akin to that between an employer and employee."

The defendant who had been found vicariously liable sought to establish that a co-defendant should also be vicariously liable. In other words, that there should be dual vicarious liability. Since the co-defendant did not have any practical control, the Supreme Court considered whether May LJ's or Rix LJ's reasoning in the *Viasystems* case was to be preferred. The Court endorsed Rix LJ reasoning and dual vicarious liability was established.

Interestingly, Lord Phillips helpfully said that there was a simpler analysis that lead to the conclusion that stage 1 was satisfied:

Provided that a brother was acting for the common purpose of the brothers as an unincorporated association, the relationship between them would be sufficient to satisfy stage 1, just as in the case of the action of a member of a partnership. Had one of the brothers injured a pedestrian when negligently driving a vehicle owned by the Institute in order to collect groceries for the community few would question that the Institute was vicariously liable for his tort.

COX V MINISTRY OF JUSTICE [2016] UKSC 10

Cox concerned a claim for personal injury by the Catering Manager of a prison arising out of the negligence of a prisoner working in the prison kitchen. The Supreme Court took stock and answered the first question of the two-stage test in the light of the judgement in *the Christian Brothers' case*.

Lord Reid confirmed:

> *the scope of vicarious liability depends on the answer to two questions. First what sort of relationship has to exist between an individual and a defendant before the defendant can be made vicariously liable in tort for the conduct of that individual? Secondly, in what manner does the conduct of that individual have to be related to that relationship, in order for vicarious liability to be imposed on the defendant?*

The judge at first instance had decided the relationship between the prison service and the prisoner was not akin to employment and so no vicarious liability could attach. Although there were a number of similarities, the prison service was legally required to offer work to prisoners and to pay them for it. This was a question of penal policy rather than a situation where the prison service and the prisoner had reached a voluntary agreement similar to the relationship of employer and employee to further the business undertaking of the prison.

The Court of Appeal disagreed, after reviewing the criteria set out by Lord Phillips at paragraph 35 of *the Christian Brothers case*. McCombe LJ observed that the work performed by prisoners in the kitchen was essential to the running of the prison. If the prisoners did not do it then someone else would have to be engaged to do so. Furthermore, although the prisoners were bound to the prison service by their sentence rather than a contract of employment, and the prisoners wages were nominal, *if anything the relationship was closer than one of employment; it was founded not on mutuality but on compulsion.*

The Supreme Court agreed. Lord Reed held:

> *In the present case, the requirements laid down in the Christian Brothers' case are met. The prison service carried on activities in furtherance of its aims. The fact that those aims are not commercially motivated but serve the public interest, is no bar to the imposition of vicarious liability. Prisoners working in the prison kitchens… are integrated into the operation of the prison, so that the activities assigned to them by the prison service form an integral part of the activities which it carries on in furtherance of its aims: in particular the activity of producing meals for prisoners. They are placed by the prison service in a position where there is a risk that they may commit a variety of negligent acts within the field of activities assigned to them. That is recognised by the health and safety training they receive. Furthermore, they work under the direction of prison staff. Mrs Cox was injured as a result of negligence by Mr Inder in carrying out the activities assigned to him. The prison service is therefore vicariously liable to her.*

At paragraph 29 Lord Reed pointed out:

> *It is important.... to understand that the general approach which Lord Phillips described is not confined to some special category of cases such as the sexual abuse of children. It is intended to provide a basis for identifying the circumstances in which vicarious liability may in principle be imposed outside the relationships of employment.*

ARMES V NOTTINGHAMSHIRE COUNTY COUNCIL [2017] UKSC 60

Cox was affirmed in *Armes* in 2017.

The claimant was physically, emotionally and sexually abused by two different sets of foster parents while in their care. The local authority had placed her in care in accordance with its statutory duty.

It was conceded that the abuse of the child was a tort for which vicarious liability could be imposed, if the relationship between the local authority and the foster parent was one that could give rise to vicarious liability. In other words, the case considered the answer to the first question of the two stage test.

Males J had considered the five features at paragraph 35 of *the Christian Brothers case*. He found that the first and fourth features were present: the local authority had the means to compensate the claimant and it had also created the risk of abuse by putting the claimant into the care of foster parents. However, he considered the remaining features were not satisfied. He regarded the foster parents as providing family life to the claimant. They were not doing this on behalf of the Council. Nor were they doing this as part of the business activity of the Council. Furthermore, the Council had little or no control over the foster parents. He considered the lack of control to be decisive.

The Court of Appeal agreed. There was a complete absence of control over day to day family routine. The control retained by the authority was at the *higher or macro level* as opposed to *micro management of the day to day family environment.*

When giving judgement in the Supreme Court, Lord Reed made reference to what was said at paragraph 21 of his judgement in Cox:-

> *The fifth of the factors – that the tortfeasor will, to a greater or lesser degree, have been under the control of the defendant – no longer has the significance that it was sometimes considered to have in the past, as Lord Phillips PSC [in the Christian Brothers case] immediately made clear. As he explained in paragraph 36, the ability to direct how an individual did his work was sometimes regarded as an important test of the existence of a relationship of master and servant, and came to be treated at times as the test for the imposition of vicarious liability. But it is not realistic in modern life to look for a right to direct how an employee should perform his duties as a necessary element in the relationship between employer and employee; nor was it in times gone by, if one thinks for example of the degree of control which the owner of a ship could have exercised over the master while the ship was at sea. Accordingly, as Lord Phillips PSC stated,* ***the significance of control is that the defendant can direct what the tortfeasor does, not how he does it.*** [Emphasis added.]

Lord Reed found that the local authority had a statutory duty to care for children who had been committed to its care, so that looking after children was part of its business. *In order to discharge that duty, insofar as it involved the provision of accommodation, maintenance and daily care, they recruited, selected and trained persons who were willing to accommodate, maintain and look after children in their homes as foster parents, and inspected their homes before any placement was made.* The authority paid them allowances and provided them with equipment. It provided them with training and the foster parents were expected to co-operate with local authority social workers with whom they had meetings at least once a month. The local authority involved the foster parents in their decision-making and required them to co-operate with arrangements for contact with the children's families. He found that foster parents were not carrying on an independent business of their own…

> *the foster parents provided care to the child as an integral part of the local authority's organisation of its childcare services… the torts committed against the claimant were committed by the foster parents in the course of an activity carried on for the benefit of the local authority.*

Finally, in relation to control:

> *although the foster parents controlled the organisation and management of their household to the extent permitted by the relevant law and practice, and dealt with most aspects of the daily care of the children without immediate supervision, it would be mistaken to regard them as being in much the same position as ordinary parents. The local authority exercises powers of approval, inspection, supervision and removal without any par-*

allel in ordinary family life. By virtue of those powers, the local authority exercised a significant degree of control over both what the foster parents did and how they did it, in order to ensure that the children's needs were met.

Lord Reed went on to explain:

it is not necessary for there to be micro-management or any high degree of control, in order to for vicarious liability to be imposed. There are countless cases where vicarious liability has been imposed for torts committed by professional persons who carry out work without close supervision.

He made reference to *E* and the *Christian Brothers* case as recent examples of the imposition of vicarious liability in the absence of micro management.

The appeal was allowed. However Lord Hughes dissented.

He focussed on two criteria: integration and control and considered that neither criteria was satisfied on the facts. Family and friends might be appointed to foster children in which case they would be subjected to the same supervisory regime as "ordinary" foster parents. There were clearly good policy reasons for ensuring that the Council could not be vicariously liable for family members. Furthermore it would be artificial to view them as being integrated into the business of the Council and subject to its control. They were fostering for the benefit of the family. He went on to say:

> *what the local authority does, in all cases, whether involving family, friends or strangers, is to take responsibility for decisions about where the children shall live, and then monitoring the progress with a view to changing the arrangements if they do not benefit the children.... The foster carers do not do what the authority would otherwise do for itself; they do something different by providing an upbringing as part of a family.*

Lord Reed made it clear that a different decision would have been reached if the abuse had been perpetrated by the child's parents since their relationship with the local authority would not have been the same. He said:

> *they would not have been recruited, selected or trained by the local authority so as to enable it to discharge its childcare functions. They would have been carrying on an activity (raising their own child) which was much more clearly distinguishable from, and independent of, the child care services carried out by the local authority than the care of unrelated children by foster parents recruited for that purpose.*

The criteria for deciding whether the relationship is one to which vicarious liability applies also provides a great deal of room for manoeuvre on the facts, as is apparent from the case set out below.

BARCLAYS BANK PLC V VARIOUS CLAIMANTS [2018] EWCA CIV 1670

The bank was held vicariously liable for assaults perpetrated by a self-employed GP during medical examinations carried out for the benefit of the bank on female employees and prospective employees. The purpose of the examinations was to assess their fitness to work and their eligibility for life insurance. The judge at first instance considered the five questions set out in paragraph 35 of the judgement in the *Christian Brothers* case. Importantly, the GP carried out the examinations in compliance with a detailed list of questions provided by the bank, that included chest measurement. After the examination he completed a form headed Barclay's Confidential Medical Report.

The appellant relied on the old distinction of employee and independent contractor and argued that the law remained that no vicarious liability could attach to independent contractors as such. It was suggested that vicarious liability might attach for assaults committed during examinations by medico-legal experts if the decision were to be upheld. Irwin LJ said:

> *It may be helpful to contrast the facts of this case, with a more usual medical examination conducted on behalf of others. Lord Faulks specifically raised the issue of deliberate torts by experts in litigation. It seems to me that even brief consideration will reveal obvious distinctions. It will be relatively rare for such an expert to conduct a general health examination, and rarer to do so against a standard formula adopted by the commissioning party....it will be rare for such examinations to be other than on a particular part of the body or a particular facet of mental health, and in all such cases the commissioning party will normally not be in a position to specify the particular tests, results or modes of physical examination to be performed. This does not seem to me to be a particularly helpful comparison, and it seems doubtful that the necessary degree of control over the medical expert would often be found. In the end this matter turns on the particular facts...*

Moreover, it seems clear to me that, adopting the approach of the Supreme Court, there will indeed by cases of independent contractors where vicarious liability will be established. Changes in the structures of employment, and of contracts for the provision of services are widespread. Operations intrinsic to a business enterprise are routinely performed by independent contractors, over long periods, accompanied by precise obligations and high levels of control. Such patterns are evidence in widely different fields of enterprise from construction, to manufacture to the services sector.

It is clearly understandable that a "bright line " test, such as is said to be the status of independent contractor would make easier the conduct of business for parties and their insurers. However, ease of business cannot displace or circumvent the principles now established by the Supreme Court. Lord Faulks advanced the status of self-employed independent contractors as representing a "coherent principle of law" thereby seeking to justify the maintenance of such a principle. The submission may be attractive at first blush. However, as has now become tolerably clear from the fields of employment and taxation law, establishing whether an individual is an employee or a self-employed independent contractor can be full of complexity and of evidential pitfalls. In my view the Cox/Mohamud questions will often represent no more challenging a basis for analysing the facts given in a case.

CONCLUSION

In considering whether a wrongdoer is an employee, a broader question may need to be answered:

> *Is the relationship between the "employer" and the wrongdoer capable of giving rise to vicarious liability?*

CHAPTER THREE
NEGLIGENCE – STAGE TWO OF THE TWO STAGE TEST

But if he was going on a frolic of his own, without being at all on his master's business, the master will not be liable.
– Per Parke B, *Joel v Morrison* (1834) 6 C and P 501

INTRODUCTION

Factors to be considered when answering stage two of the test depend on whether the wrongdoing is negligent or an intentional tort. In this chapter stage two is considered in cases of negligence.

If the individual is a clear – cut employee, stage one of the test is satisfied. The relationship of employer and employee is one where vicarious liability may attach. The next question is whether the wrongdoing occurred in the course of employment. It is important to bear in mind there will be no vicarious liability unless all the necessary elements of the employee's wrongdoing occur in the course of employment.

The starting point for any consideration of the vicarious liability of an employer is *Salmond Law of Torts 1st ed. (1907) page 8.* A wrongful act is deemed to be done in the course of employment if:

> "*it is either (1) a wrongful act authorised by the master, or (2) a wrongful and unauthorised mode of doing some act authorised by the master. It is clear that the master is responsible for acts actually authorised by him: for liability would exist in*

> *this case, even if the relation between the parties was merely one of agency, and not one of service at all.* ***But a master, as opposed to the employer of an independent contractor, is liable for acts even which he has not authorised, provided they are so connected with acts that he has authorised that they may rightly be regarded as modes – although improper modes – of doing them."*** [Emphasis added.]

The critical question is whether the employee is acting inside or outside the authority of his employer, or whether he is acting within his authority in a way that has been unauthorised. If he is acting outside the authority of his employer, he is doing something he is not employed to do and his employer is not vicariously liable for his negligence. If he is acting inside his employer's authority, even if it is in an improper way, vicarious liability will attach.

Where the wrongdoer is not an employee, but there is a relationship akin to employment so that vicarious liability may attach, the question to be answered is:

> *Is there a sufficiently close connection between the wrongdoing and the relationship between the "employer" and the wrongdoer?*

See Lord Phillips in the *Christian Brothers case* at paragraph 21.

This test is based on the last sentence of the Salmond test, set out above.

NEGLIGENT EMPLOYEES

Many of the cases relevant to authority are old driving cases, some of which concern vicarious liability for acts of employees that the employer has expressly prohibited.

In *Century Insurance Company Limited v Northern Ireland Road Transport Board* [1942] AC 509, the House of Lords held that the employer was vicariously liable for the acts of a lorry driver who caused an explosion while delivering petrol from his lorry into a storage tank in the course of his employment. After lighting a cigarette he threw away a match that started a fire. This was simply an improper way of carrying out the task.

In 1946 a man was killed in a road traffic accident while being driven as a passenger in a van. The driver's employer had forbidden the driver from carrying passengers such as the deceased. The deceased had been aware of this. The driver had told him on a previous occasion that he took the lift at his own risk. Furthermore there was a sign on the outside of the van that prohibited unauthorised passengers. His widow brought a claim for damages on behalf of herself and her two young children against the driver's employer. The Court of Appeal held that the deceased was in the van as a trespasser. Although the driver had been driving the van on a route that was within the course of his employment, that employment did not extend to giving a lift to someone in defiance of his employer's prohibition. *He was doing something that he had no right whatsoever to do, and qua the deceased man he was as much on a frolic of his own as if he had been driving somewhere on some amusement of his own quite unauthorised by his employers.* Per the Master of the Rolls Lord Greene in *Twine v Bean's Express Limited* The Times Law Reports 12 July 1946.

In 1946 no duty of care was ever owed to trespassers. If a pedestrian had been injured in the collision, he would have had a cause of action against the driver, although the deceased did not.

A totally unauthorised journey by a driver on business of his own will take him outside the course of his employment. However the extent of the detour is relevant. Can it be considered a separate journey distinct from what the employee is employed to do? For example:

> *when there are passengers whom the servant on this master's behalf has taken on board for transport to Glasgow, their transport and safety does not cease at a certain stage of the journey to be the master's business, or part of his enterprise merely because the servant has for his own purposes chosen some route which is contrary to his instructions.*
>
> – per Lord Pearce in *A & W Hemphill Ltd v Williams* [1966] Vol 2 page 101 Lloyds List Law Reports.

In *London County Council v Cattermoles (Garages) Limited* [1953] 1 WLR 997 the Court of Appeal found a garage vicariously liable for the negligence of a general hand employed on various duties, including pushing cars out of the way to prevent obstructions. He had been forbidden to drive since he did not have a license. When instructed to move a van that was preventing access to the defendant's petrol pumps, he drove it off the forecourt onto the road instead of pushing it out of the way. A collision occurred. It was held that what the garage hand did was simply a wrongful or unauthorised mode of doing an act authorised by the defendant, despite the express prohibition. The prohibition against moving cars by driving them did not amount to such a limitation on the general hand's authority to move vehicles out of the way that he was doing something outside his employment when driving the car.

Willmer LJ clearly described the principle to be applied in prohibition cases in *Ilkiw v Samuels* [1963] 1 W.L.:

> *...the mere fact that the act complained of was done in disobedience to express instructions is of no necessary materiality in deciding whether the act was in the course of employment... Once again, as is not uncommon, the difficulty is to apply the principle to the unusual facts of the case.*

In *Kay v ITW Limited* [1968] 1QB 140 a fork lift truck driver, who was also authorised to drive a van, moved a five ton lorry that did not belong to his employer in order to gain access to a warehouse. He injured a fellow employee as a result of his negligent driving. There was no urgency and the driver of the lorry, who was present and one of his employer's customers, could have been asked to move it. The trial judge found driver's employers vicariously liable for his negligence. On appeal, the defendant employer argued:

> *that to enter the cab of a visiting lorry, particularly of a large lorry with a diesel engine of which he had apparently no knowledge or experience, and to set it in motion was such an extreme, unforeseeable and dangerous thing to do that it ought not to be held to be incidental to the work for which Ord* [the driver] *was employed, and that an accident resulting therefrom ought not to bring liability to his employers.*

The Court of Appeal held that the forklift truck driver's employers were vicariously liable for his negligence. He was not simply attempting to drive another person's vehicle which, looked at in isolation from the circumstances, would not have been within the course of his employment. He was seeking to remove an obstruction that prevented him from fulfilling his task of returning the forklift truck. However the conduct was so exceptional and excessive that it was near the borderline.

Danckwerts LJ expressed considerable sympathy for the employer, as he dismissed the appeal:

> *When one considers the position in this way of the vicarious liability of employers and the provisions of the Factories Act 1961, it seems to me that the employer's life is a somewhat hazardous one. Indeed, it appears that it would be a good deal safer to keep lions or other wild animals in a park than to engage in a business involving the employment of labour.*

One wonders what he would have to say now, fifty years later?

In 1975 a thirteen-year-old boy, paid by a milkman to help him with delivering and collecting milk bottles, was injured when he fell off the milk float as a result of the milkman's negligent driving. The boy brought an action for damages against the milkman's employer. It defended the claim by arguing the milkman had been prohibited from employing young persons to assist him with his duties and so he had been acting outside his employment when the accident occurred. Lord Denning and the Court of Appeal found for the plaintiff. The prohibition did not define the parameters of the employment. It affected only the conduct of the employment. Lord Denning MR explained:

> *...this case falls within those in which the prohibition affects only the conduct within the sphere of the employment and did not take the conduct outside the sphere altogether.*

In disregarding the prohibition the milkman was still engaged on his employer's business: *Rose v Plenty* [1976]1 W.L.R 141

Employees arriving at their place of work will generally be regarded as within the course of employment from when they arrive at work until they leave, providing they arrive neither unreasonably early or leave unreasonably late. In *Compton v McClure* [1975] ICR 379, an employer was vicariously liable for the negligent driving of its employee who had driven through the gates of the employer's premises and was driving too fast in order to clock on duty on time.

A useful rule of thumb to be applied subject to the particular circumstances of the case: travelling from home to and from the place of work does not fall within employment, unless the person is travelling to a place of work other than his usual place of work. Travelling between different places of work does fall within the course of employment.

In *Smith v Stages and another* 1 AC 1989 the House of Lords held an employee who was paid wages by his employer to travel from his ordinary residence to a place other than his usual workplace to carry out a job and was also paid wages for the return journey home was acting in the course of employment while travelling. The fact the employee might have discretion as to the mode and time of travel did not take the journey out of the course of employment.

In an interesting case from 1976 a police constable was injured in a football match when playing in his force team against another police force. He made a claim for industrial injuries benefits. The National Insurance Commissioner rejected the claim since he found that participation in sports was not " in the course of his employment" within the meaning of the relevant legislation. The Court of Appeal agreed that football was not work which the claimant was employed to do: *R v National Insurance Comp ex parte Michael* [1977] 1 WLR 109. Two members of the Court of Appeal made it clear that the case was not authority for the proposition that playing football could *never* be an activity arising in the course of a police constable's duty.

Even before the law of vicarious liability went on the move with *Lister* in 2002 (see next chapter), it was clear that the employers of full-time professionals may be vicariously liable for their negligent acts, even though they have little or no control over the way they carry out their tasks. Examples include the liability of hospitals for the negligence of their doctors, and the liability of local authorities for the negligence of their teachers.

NEGLIGENT NON-EMPLOYEES WITH RELATIONSHIP AKIN TO EMPLOYMENT

In cases where the relationship between the defendant and the tortfeasor is *akin to employment* the test is the same as where the relationship is one of employment in the strict sense. In the *Christian Brothers* case Lord Phillips said:

> *where the tortfeasor does what he is required or requested to do pursuant to his relationship with the defendant in a manner that is negligent stage 2 of the test is likely to be satisfied.*

See the facts of the *Viasystems* case to which reference is made in the last chapter.

CONCLUSION

Although the law of vicarious liability has evolved significantly in the last sixteen years, the developments are largely restricted to intentional torts. Older cases may remain helpful when assessing whether an employer is likely to be liable for an employee's negligence.

CHAPTER FOUR
INTENTIONAL TORTS – ASSAULT – STAGE TWO OF THE TWO STAGE TEST

Vicarious liability is a principle of strict liability... This consideration underlines the need to keep the doctrine within clear limits....

– Lord Steyn in *Barnard v Attorney General of Jamaica* [2004]

INTRODUCTION

In cases of intentional torts, the test in the first edition of Salmond Law of Torts has been critical. By way of reminder, the last part of the test is set out below:

> *But a master, as opposed to the employer of an independent contractor, is liable for acts even which he has not authorised, provided they are so connected with acts that he has authorised that they may rightly be regarded as modes – although improper modes – of doing them."*

Leading cases from 2002 onwards have confirmed that a broad approach is to be adopted to deciding what acts the master has authorised, in line with Lord Denning's decision in *Rose v Plenty* [1976]1 W.L.R 141: see the preceding chapter on Negligence. The elements of a person's employment are not to be deconstructed so as to identify individually what acts have been authorised. Instead, one stands back and looks at the parameters of the employment in the round. But how round is round? Or how broad is broad?

DEVELOPMENT OF THE LAW

Patrick Fennelly v Connex South Eastern Limited [2001] IRLR 390 was decided by the Court of Appeal shortly before *Lister v Hedley Hall* [2002] 1 AC 215 and the law going on the move. The facts concerned an assault by a ticket inspector on a rude travelling member of the public at a railway station. The passenger had initially refused to show the inspector his ticket since he had already produced it to another inspector at the ticket barrier. He eventually did so and the inspector handed the ticket back to him. The passenger started to walk away in the direction of the station platform, when the ticket inspector said: *I have had enough of this.* With that he grabbed him from behind, in a headlock, and dragged him down some stairs, causing him injury. The trial judge decided that the train operating company was not vicariously liable for the assault since the inspector had checked the ticket and the claimant was going on his way when the assault was carried out.

> *He had fulfilled and concluded his authorised role. He had become personally angry and was pursuing his own ends. The defendants cannot be said to be vicariously liable for that. He was doing nothing that he was authorised to do. He was not going about his employer's business but his own.*

The claimant appealed.

The Court of Appeal allowed the appeal. The trial judge had adopted too narrow an approach. There was too precise a focus on authorisation. Buxton LJ held:

> *I consider it artificial to say that just because* [the claimant] *was walking on, what happened next – immediately next – was divorced from what* [the inspector] *was employed to do. The neck lock sprang directly out of the altercation…impossible in my view to say that the course of employment had been departed from and had come to an end at the very moment, the brief second of time, when* [the claimant] *walked away.*

In reaching his decision the judge was assisted by Comyn J's test in *Harrison v Michelin Tyre Co* [1985] 1 All ER 918: *Was it* [the wrongful act] *so divergent from the employment as to be plainly alien to and wholly distinguishable from the employment?* The question was to be determined by asking whether a reasonable man looking at all the circumstances would think that the incident was part and parcel of the employment.

The judge distinguished *Daniels v Whetstone Entertainments and Allender* [1962] 2 Lloyds Rep 1, where there had been an altercation between a steward and a customer of a dance hall. Two assaults followed. The employer was vicariously liable for the first assault carried out by the steward on a customer in the dance hall. It was not so liable for the second assault carried out outside the dance hall after the customer had left. The court relied on the fact the manager had followed the steward outside and told him in no uncertain terms to come back inside and get on with his duties. Instead, he assaulted the customer again. Buxton LJ said:

> *Leaving aside all the questions of authority and prohibition, that intervention on the part of the manager, added to the fact that, effectively, the original row had calmed down and the steward was seeking to revenge himself, makes the case quite different from a case such as the present; it marked a clear divide between the assault that involved acting in his employment and the assault which did not.*

It is only since the Police Act 1964 that Chief Constables have been held vicariously liable for the wrongdoing of their officers. Under section 88 (1) of the Police Act 1998 (replacing the Police Act 1964):-

> *The chief officer of police for a police area shall be liable in respect of any unlawful conduct of constables under his direction and control in the performance or* ***purported performance*** *of their functions in like manner as a master is liable in respect of any unlawful conduct of his servants in the course of their employment, and accordingly shall in the case of a tort, be treated for all purposes as a joint tortfeasor.* [Emphasis added]

In *Weir v Bettison (sued as Chief Constable of Merseyside)* [2003] EWCA Civ 111, an off duty police officer had borrowed a marked police van without permission in order to help his girlfriend to move house. While unloading the van he had an argument with the claimant who was suspected of rifling through his girlfriend's belongings. The police officer manhandled him into the police van where he assaulted him. He told him he would take him to the police station, but released him when it became clear that nothing had been stolen.

It is arguable that the liability of a chief constable is more extensive than the vicarious liability of an employer and reference was made to this by the Right Honourable Sir Dennis Henry who said:-

> *To establish liability the claimant has to show more than the mere fact that the tortfeasor was a police officer. He has to show that the tort he alleges was committed at a time when the police officer was apparently acting in his capacity as a constable. It seems to me that from the moment PC Dudley started to put Weir out of the building he was apparently exercising his authority as a constable.*

In a case decided later the same year Lord Justice Judge described the facts as *stark.* In *Donald Wilson Mattis v Gerard Pollock (T/A Flamingo's Nightclub)* [2003] EWCV Civ 887 the claimant was stabbed by a doorman employed by the defendant at its nightclub and rendered paraplegic. The doorman was convicted of grievous bodily harm with intent and sentenced to a term of eight years imprisonment. He was unlicensed and the defendant was subsequently convicted of employing him as an unlicensed door supervisor.

The stabbing occurred outside the nightclub, after an altercation inside it when the claimant went to the aid of a customer who was being beaten up by the doorman. The doorman was set upon by other customers and forced to flee. This was an event which had wholly undermined his status and what the defendant employer expected him to be. The doorman had returned to his flat 500 yards away in order to collect a knife. On his way back to the club he had stabbed the claimant who was waiting on a street corner, about to make his way home.

The claimant maintained the defendant was vicariously liable for the stabbing since it happened in the course of the doorman's employment at the club. The claimant also alleged that the defendant was in breach of its duty of care to him personally. The defendant avoided liability at trial and the claimant appealed.

The appeal was successful, largely because the defendant had encouraged the doorman's aggressive behaviour and should not have employed him without a license. The judge had not sufficiently addressed the fact that the doorman *was encouraged and expected to perform his duties in an aggressive and intimidatory manner, which included physical manhandling of customers....The whole point of any physical confrontation with* [the defendant's] *customers in the nightclub .... was that he should win it.*

Moreover, the stabbing formed part of the original altercation. Lord Justice Judge held:

> *The stabbing of Mr Mattis represented the unfortunate and virtual culmination of the unpleasant incident which had started within the club, and could not fairly and justly be treated in isolation from earlier events, or as a separate and distinct incident,*

He noted that vicarious liability did not necessarily point to a primary duty of care owed by the nightclub to the claimant. However, he thought such a duty was likely on the facts of this case.

The focus returned to the police in *Clinton Barnard v the Attorney General of Jamaica* [2004] UKPC 47 decided by the Privy Council in favour of the claimant. The facts were similarly stark.

After waiting his turn in a long queue at the Central Sorting Office in Kingston, the claimant picked up the telephone and dialled the number for an overseas call. Suddenly a man intervened, announced "police" and demanded the phone. The claimant refused to release the phone at which point the man said "boy me naw join no line, give me the phone". The constable slapped the claimant on the hand and shoved him in his chest. As the claimant continued to refuse he then:

> *"took two steps backwards, pulled out his service revolver, pointed it at the plaintiff, and fired at his head at point blank range. The bullet hit the plaintiff to the left side of his head, leaving entry and exit wounds in the skull. ...In the hospital Constable Morgan placed the plaintiff under arrest for allegedly assaulting a police officer and handcuffed him to his bed."*

By the time of the trial Constable Morgan had left the island and successfully disappeared.

In Jamaica a constable is an employee of the Crown. The practice was to allow police officers take loaded firearms home and carry them while off duty. The defendant pleaded that the shooting was carried out entirely for the constable's own benefit and he was not acting in the course of his employment or for his employer's benefit.

The trial judge decided that the Attorney General was vicariously liable for the acts of the officer. The Court of Appeal reversed this decision and the claimant appealed to the Privy Council.

In reaching its decision the Privy Council assumed the officer was not on duty and that the shooting occurred outside his immediate area of responsibility. It also assumed that the constable demanded to be allowed to make a private call, although it was not clear whether he wanted to make the call as part of his police function.

Lord Steyn noted that the principles enunciated in <u>*Lister*</u>, which he had promulgated in the House of Lords two years earlier, for which see the next chapter headed sexual abuse, were of general application to intentional torts. He stated:

> *Vicarious liability is a principle of strict liability... This consideration underlines the need to keep the doctrine within clear limits....*
>
> *...the Board is firmly of the view that the policy rationale on which vicarious liability is founded is not a vague notion of justice between man and man. It has clear limits......*
>
> *....the principle of vicarious liability is not infinitely extendable.*

However, there were three main points to note when applying the principles to the facts of the case, and deciding that there was a sufficiently close connection to the officer's employment for vicarious liability to attach to his employer:

1. The shooting followed immediately after the constable's announcement that he was a police officer, and it was the fact the claimant was not prepared to yield to this assertion of authority which lead to the shooting;

2. *Approaching the matter in the broad way required by <u>Lister</u>, the constable's subsequent act in arresting the claimant in the*

hospital is explicable on the basis the constable alleged that the claimant had interfered with his execution of his duties as a policeman. It is retrospectant evidence which suggests that the constable had purported to act as a policeman immediately before he shot the claimant.

3. The police authorities increased the risk by routinely allowing policemen to take loaded service revolvers home and to carry them while off duty. *It does not follow that the using of a service revolver by a policeman would without more make the police authority vicariously liable. That would be going too far. But taking into account the dominant feature of this case, viz that the constable at all material times purported to act as a policeman, the risks created by the police authorities reinforce the conclusion that vicarious liability is established.*

In *Gravil v Redruth Rugby Football Club* [2008] EWCA Civ 689, the Court of Appeal confirmed the club was vicariously liable for a punch thrown by one of its players at the end of a match. The contract of employment between the player and the club expressly stated that the player should not physically assault an opponent and noted that the club might be vicariously liable for such actions. The punch had been thrown during a melee of a kind that often occurred in rugby matches, even after the whistle had blown. Although the punch was thrown during a melee shortly after the match had ended, it was part of the game and not independent of it. There was a very close connection between the punch and player's employment as a footballer for it to be fair and just to hold the club vicariously liable, in accordance with the test set out by Lord Steyn in *Lister*.

When giving judgement Sir Anthony Clarke MR, made it clear that once a close connection has been established, and the punch was a reasonably incidental risk of playing rugby pursuant to the contract, the court should then go on to consider whether it would be fair and just to hold the employer vicariously liable, in accordance with *Lister*. On the facts of this case the punch was so closely connected with the wrongdoer's employment that it would be fair and just to hold the club liable.

The Court of Appeal was at pains to make clear there would have been no vicarious liability in the absence of a contract of employment, and so the decision is not relevant to sporting events where players are not under contract.

Weddall v Barchester Healthcare Limited and *Wallbank v Wallbank Fox Designs Limited* [2012] EWCA Civ 25 were a conjoined appeal four years later, arising out of assaults on managers in response to a request and an instruction respectively.

In the first case a drunken and off duty Senior Health Assistant employed by the defendant care home refused his manager's request to cover for a member of staff who had called in sick. The assistant was at home when the manager telephoned with the suggestion. After refusing to come in to work he bicycled to the home and, without words or further ado, assaulted the manager who was sitting at the front of the home. The trial judge held there was no vicarious liability and the Court of Appeal agreed. Lord Justice Pill had

> *...no difficulty in concluding that the judge had reached the right conclusion for the right reasons. The violence was the employee's response to a routine and proper request that he*

> *volunteer for a night shift. When he received the request, Marsh* [the claimant] *was* [off duty] *and at home. He got on his bicycle, in a drunken state, and rode to the workplace with the purpose of inflicting serious violence on Weddall. He attacked Weddall twenty minutes after receiving* [and refusing] *the request* [to work a night shift]. *That was an independent venture of Marsh's own, separate and distinct from Marsh's employment as a Senior Healthcare Assistant at a care home. As the judge put it, Marsh was "acting personally for his own reasons". The instruction, or request as it in fact was, was no more than a pretext for an act of violence unconnected with work as a health assistant. ... it is of course an irony that it is the outrageousness of Marsh's conduct that deprives Weddall of a remedy against his employer but the doctrine of vicarious liability, which is policy based, must be kept within limits.*

The appeal in *Wallbank* was successful. In that case the claimant was Managing Director and one of six employees employed by the defendant, a small company that manufactured bedframes. He reprimanded a powder coater for his delay in putting bedframes onto the conveyor belt to a heating oven. The claimant then went to assist the powder coater with loading the bedframes, saying "come on". In response to this instruction the employee threw him into a table, breaking a vertebra in his lower back. Lord Pill held:

> ... *The possibility of friction is inherent in any employment relationship but particularly one in a factory, even a small factory, where instant instructions and quick reactions are required. Frustrations leading to a reaction involving some violence are predictable. The risk of an over-robust reaction to*

an instruction is a risk created by employment. It may be reasonably incidental to the employment rather than unrelated to or independent of it.

In the course of giving judgement he helpfully clarified:

there can, in my judgement, be no strict distinction between violence towards a third party and violence towards a fellow employee. When considering vicarious liability the same factors operate in both situations....

More importantly he said:

Mr Cleeve [for the claimant] *puts it broadly: an employee who reacts to an instruction with violence towards the instructing employee is inevitably acting in the course of his employment. To accept that proposition would, in my judgement, be to go too far. The policy reasons for limiting the operation of the principle of vicarious liability are sound.*

Lord Justice Aitkens confirmed:

It would be unwise for this court to attempt to identify any one of the expression or concepts that have begun previously used by this court or the House of Lords or Privy Council as embodying the definitive test of when a tort was committed by the employee tortfeasor in the course of his employment. The various different formulations have to be considered in the context of the particular facts of the case in hand.

MOHAMUD V WM MORRISON SUPERMARKETS PLC

In *Mohamud v WM Morrison Supermarkets plc* [2016] UKSC 11 Lord Toulson set out the facts as follows:

The claimant was of Somali origin. On the morning of 15 March 2008 he was on his way to take part with other members of his community in an event in London. While he was at the defendant's petrol station in Birmingham he decided to inquire whether it would be possible to print some documents from a USB stick he was carrying.

The claimant went into the kiosk and explained to the staff what he wanted. There were two or three staff present. Mr Khan who was behind the counter replied by saying: "We don't do such shit". The claimant protested at being spoken to in that manner. Using foul, racist and threatening language Mr Khan ordered the claimant to leave. The claimant walked out of the kiosk and returned to his car by the air pump. He was followed by Mr Khan. The claimant got into his car and switched on the engine, but before he could drive off Mr Khan opened the front passenger door and told him in threatening words never to come back. The claimant told Mr Khan to get out of the car and shut the passenger door. Instead, Mr Khan punched him on the left temple causing him pain and shock. The claimant switched off the engine and got out in order to walk round and close the passenger door. At this point Mr Khan again punched him in the head, knocked him to the floor and subjected him to a serious attack, involving punches and kicks, while the claimant lay curled up on the petrol station forecourt, trying to protect his head from the blows. In carrying out the attack Mr Khan ignored instructions from his supervisor, who came on the scene at some stage and tried to stop Mr Khan from behaving as he did. The judge concluded that the reasons for Mr Khan's behaviour were a matter of speculation. The claimant himself had said and done nothing which could be considered abusive or aggressive.

Applying the test set out in *Lister* (see chapter five) the question was whether Mr Khan's wrongdoing was so closely connected with his employment to make it just to impose vicarious liability on Morrison.

The trial judge decided it was not and so did the Court of Appeal. Lord Toulson referred to the Court of Appeal's judgement in the following terms:

Mr Khan's duties were circumscribed. He was not given duties involving a clear possibility of confrontation or placed in a situation where an outbreak of violence was likely. The fact that his employment involved interaction with customers was not enough to make his employers liable for his use of violence towards the claimant... Christopher Clarke LJ said that he was attracted for a time by the proposition that the assault could be looked at as a perverse execution of Mr Khan's duty to engage with customers, but he considered that such an approach parted company with reality.

The claimant clearly considered there was some substance to this approach. In his appeal to the Supreme Court he invited the Court to abandon the close connection test in favour of a new broader test:

> *representative capacity. In the case of a tort committed by an employee, the decisive question should be whether a reasonable observer would consider the employee to be acting in the capacity of a representative of the employer at the time of committing the tort.*

Alternatively, it was argued the claimant should have succeeded because he was a lawful visitor to the premises and:

> *Mr Khan was acting within the* ***field of activities*** *assigned to him in dealing with the claimant* [emphasis added].

Lord Toulson reviewed the authorities, going back as far as the reign of Henry IV, and identified the principle of social justice enunciated by Holt CJ as underlying the liability of masters for the wrongdoing of their servants (above). He noted that:

> *…Salmond's formulation was not universally satisfactory. The difficulties in its application were particularly evident in cases of injury to persons or property caused by an employee's deliberate act of misconduct.*

He affirmed the decision in *Warren v Henlys Limited* [1948] 2 All ER 935 where a customer at a petrol station had an angry confrontation with a petrol station attendant, who wrongly suspected him of trying to make off without payment. The customer became enraged at the manner in which he was spoken to by the attendant. After paying for the petrol, the customer saw a passing police car and drove off after it. He complained to the police officer about the attendant's conduct and persuaded the officer to return with him to the police station. The officer listened to both men and indicated that he did not think that it was a police matter, whereupon the customer said that he would report the attendant to his employer. The officer was on the point of leaving, when the attendant punched the claimant in the face, knocking him to the ground. The employer was not vicariously liable for the petrol station attendant. By the time the assault happened the customer's business with the petrol station had ended, the petrol had been paid for and the customer had left the premises. When he returned with the police officer it was for the purpose of making a personal complaint about the attendant.

Lord Toulson considered a New Zealand case with approval: *Petterson v Royal Oak Hotel Limited* [1948] NZLR 136. He described it thus: a barman refused to serve a drunken customer with more alcohol. As the customer was on is way out of the premises, he threw a glass at the barman which broke in pieces at his feet. The barman picked up a piece of the broken glass and threw it back at the departing customer, but missed him and injured the eye of another customer, who sued for damages….The Court of Appeal held that the barman's act was an improper mode of doing his job of keeping order in the bar and avoiding altercations, although at the time the customer was leaving.

Deatons Pty Ltd v Flew (1949) 79 CLR 370, an Australian case, was wrongly decided. The claimant lost the sight of an eye when a barmaid employed by the defendant threw a glass at him. Dixon J gave two reasons for dismissing the case: *first that she did not throw the glass in the course of keeping discipline, and secondly, that she was not in charge of the bar but was working under the supervision of another woman.*

Lord Toulson said:

I agree that it was tortuous and artificial to describe the barmaid's conduct as a mode of performing what she was employed to do, but that does not make this result just. In a broader sense it occurred in the course of her employment. She was employed by the hotel proprietor to serve customers. She was approached in that capacity by a customer, and ordinary members of the public would surely expect the company who employed her to serve customers to have some responsibility for her conduct towards them. And it surely cannot be right that the measure of the company's responsibility should depend on whether she was the head barmaid or an assistant. The customer would have no knowledge of what were the exact limits of her responsibilities.

The Supreme Court refused to redefine the close connection test. Lord Toulson said:

In the simplest terms, the court has to consider two matters. The question is what functions or "field of activities" have been entrusted by the employer to the employee, or, in everyday language, what was the nature of his job. As has been emphasised in several cases, this question must be addressed broadly….

Secondly, the court must decide whether there was sufficient connection between the position in which he was employed and his wrongful conduct to make it right for the employer to be held liable under the principle of social justice which goes back to Holt. ***To try to measure the closeness of connection, as it were, on a scale of 1 to 10 would be a forlorn exercise and, what is more, would miss the point. The cases in which the necessary connection has been found for Holt's principle to***

> ***be applied are cases in which the employee used or misused the position entrusted to him in a way which injured the third party.*** [Emphasis added]

Held*:*

> *It was Mr Khan's job to attend to customers and respond to their inquiries. His conduct in answering the claimant's request in a foul-mouthed way and ordering him to leave was inexcusable but was within the field of activities assigned to him. What happened thereafter was an unbroken sequence of events. It was not right to regard Mr Khan as having metaphorically taken off his uniform when came out from behind the counter and followed the claimant onto the forecourt. He was following up on what he had said to the claimant and it was a seamless episode. Secondly, once on the forecourt, Mr Khan had told the claimant in threatening terms that he was never to come back to the petrol station. That was not something personal between him and the customer; he was ordering him to keep away from his employer's premises and he reinforced that order by violence. In doing so he was purporting to act in the furtherance of his employer's business. While it was a gross abuse of his position, it was in connection with the business in which he was employed. Since the supermarket had entrusted him with the position of serving customers, it was just that he should be held responsible for abuse of that position.*

This result may seem bizarre until one reminds oneself that no one criterion is determinative of vicarious liability. It depends on the facts. On these facts the Supreme Court ignored the (absence) of any significantly increased risk, the fact the employment seemed merely to give the perpetrator the opportunity for a racist attack, and also ignored the fact he was probably acting for his own ends. The Court placed significance on Mr Khan ordering the claimant not to come back again when he was out on the forecourt. This was regarded as evidence that he was acting in the course of his employment (despite ignoring the instructions of his supervisor). The Supreme Court expressed no concern for restricting the ambit of the principle of vicarious liability.

FROLICS, INCLUDING A FROLIC RECENTLY OVERTURNED BY THE COURT OF APPEAL

References are frequently made to *Aldred v Nacanco Limited* [1987] IRLR 292, as an example of a frolic for which no vicarious liability attached to the employer. Mr Justice Turner dismissed the claimant's claim for damages in an extempore judgement given at the end of the first morning of the trial. His decision was upheld by the Court of Appeal. An employee had jolted a slightly loose wash hand basin in order to startle the claimant, who was leaning back against the rim of the basin. The duly startled claimant had immediately turned around and injured her back in doing so. Turner J held that these actions *were something quite outside – however one cares to define the ambit of her behaviour – the scope or the context of her employment.*

In *Graham v Commercial Bodyworks Limited* [2015] EWCA Cov 47, the claimant had sustained serious injuries in the course of his employment at the defendant's body repair shop. He and a co-employee (and friend) had been messing about and chasing each other, when the co-employee lightly sprayed the claimant's overalls with highly flammable thinning agent, and then lit his cigarette lighter close by. There is a faint suggestion the perpetrator may not have been aware he was spraying thinning agent. However, the claimant's overalls had gone up in flames. The trial judge described the co-employee's actions as *a serious assault on this then friend.* The actions were deliberate and reckless as regards the risks and the description of the incident as *horseplay* was a *gross underestimate.* Nevertheless he held there was no vicarious liability and the claimant appealed, only to lose again.

In reaching a decision, Lord Justice Longmore set out the following passage from Bazely v Curry (above). Although the case concerned child sexual abuse he found the principles enunciated by McLachlin J useful.

> *It must be possible to say that the employer significantly increased the risk of harm by putting the employee in his or her position and requiring him to perform the assigned tasks. The policy considerations that justify imposition of vicarious liability for an employee's sexual misconduct are unlikely to be satisfied by incidental considerations of time and place. For example an incidental or random attack by an employee that merely happens to take place on the employer's premises during working hours will scarcely justify holding the employer liable. Such an attack is unlikely to be related to the business the employer is conducting or what the employee was asked to do and, hence, to any risk that was created.*

In other words, where the workplace simply provides the opportunity for the wrongdoing, no vicarious liability is likely to attach. Examples given in other cases include a solicitors' firm which is not vicariously liable for a clerk that steals a client's handbag. Nor will a school be vicariously liable for a gardener who commits a sexual assault. In Deatons v Pty v Flew, quoted in Lister above, an employer is not vicariously liable for a barmaid employed simply to serve customers, who assaults a customer with a glass. In _Gravil_ (above) the Master of the Rolls cast some doubt on whether this case, decided by the High Court in Australia in 1947, would be decided the same way today.

Lord Justice Longmore also found the dicta of Lord Nicholls in _Dubai Aluminium Co Ltd v Salaam_ [2003] 2 AC 366 helpful. This case is considered in more detail in the chapter headed Reliance Torts. In the meantime, Lord Nicholls had these reassuring words to say:-

> *This close connection test focuses attention in the right direction. But it affords no guidance on the type or degree of connection which will normally be regarded as sufficiently close to prompt the legal conclusion that the risk of the wrongful act occurring and any loss flowing from the wrongful act, should fall on the firm or employer rather than the person who was wronged…*
>
> *This lack of precision is inevitable, given the infinite range of circumstances where the issue arises. The crucial feature or features, either producing or negativing vicarious liability, vary widely from one case or type of case to the next. Essentially the court makes an evaluative judgement in each case, having regard to all the circumstances and, importantly, having regard also to the assistance provided by previous court decisions. In this field the latter form of assistances is particularly valuable.*

Longmore LJ made a distinction between cases where the use of reasonable force, or particular friction between employees is inherent in the employment (such as when working in a factory on a conveyor belt) and cases where:

> *normal friction in the workplace gets out of hand* or there is *uncalled for antagonism which, while occurring in the work-place, originates outside it.* In

Two Scottish cases were particularly helpful to Lord Justice Longmore when reaching his decision. In *Wilson v. Exel UK Limited* [2010] CSIH 35, a health and safety supervisor pulled the claimant's ponytail making a ribald remark as he did so. This was no more than a prank but the claimant sustained some injury. The court held that the supervisor's actions were not connected with his employment. Much reference was made to *Lister* in the judgement. Lord Carloway helpfully observed:

> *From a practical point of view, however, the ground in this case, of pranks between co-employees is well trodden. Within the context of the broad test is the well- established and fundamental principle of finding vicarious liability applicable when the actings of the employee can be said to be within the scope of his employment.*

(Vicarious liability for sex discrimination and harassment under the Equality Act 2010 might be considered by an Employment Tribunal today.)

Vaickuviene v Sainsbury PLC [2013] CSIH 67 was a murder case. A Mr McCulloch killed his fellow employee Mr Romasov in a Sainsbury's supermarket in Aberdeen, with a knife from the kitchenware aisle. The stabbing was the culmination of two days of harassment, during which Mr McCulloch had informed Mr Romasov that he did not like immigrants and advised he should go back to his own country. On the night of the killing there had been an argument when he had objected to Mr Romasov sharing a table with him. The court found there was no connection between the harassment and killing and what Mr McCulloch was employed to do in Sainsburys. *Rather, McCulloch's employment simply provided him with the opportunity to carry out his own personal campaign of harassment with tragic consequences.*

Lord Longmore followed this Scottish line of authority decided after *Lister* and held:

> *the real cause of Mr Graham's injuries was the no doubt frolicsome but reckless horseplay of Mr Wilkinson which cannot be said to have occurred in the course of employment.* The appeal was dismissed.

It was the Managing Director who assaulted his subordinate Sales Manager at a Christmas party in *Clive Bellman v Northampton Recruitment Limited* [2016] EWJC 3103, decided by the High Court after *Mohamud* below. The two had been life-long friends when the Managing Director offered the claimant the role in 2010. About a year later another person called Stephen Kelly was recruited, a month before the company's Christmas party. It was rumoured he was being paid more than anyone else and he appears to have been based at the company's Northampton office, while the claimant was based at its other office in Nuneaton.

His Honour Judge Cotter QC described the Christmas party in these terms:

> *The party was an ordinary or usual Christmas party of the type no doubt dreaded by some and an annual highlight for others. Not surprisingly alcohol was consumed by many attending.*

There were 24 guests. When the party came to an end at the Golf Club, just over half the guests went on to the Hilton Hotel. An altercation arose there after the claimant questioned the Managing Director about the appointment of Stephen Kelly. The Managing Director went on a general rant to all those present asserting it was his company and he would make the decisions. The claimant suggested in a non-aggressive manner that Stephen Kelly would be better employed at Nuneaton rather than in the Northampton office. At this the Managing Director, who was very inebriated, punched him. The claimant rose from the floor, bleeding from the area around his left eye. He held out his hands in a gesture of surrender and said "John, what are you doing? Don't do this." The Managing Director lost all control, broke free of those restraining him and punched him again. It was about 3am. The claimant suffered very severe traumatic brain injury on the second punch.

After providing a useful summary of the policy considerations and criteria that he needed to apply to these facts the judge went on to make the following findings:

1. The Christmas party and any obligation to attend it came to an end at the Golf Club. *In effect a line could be drawn under the evening's event and not surprisingly some employees went home.*

2. The conversation only turned to work matters after significant period of time spent talking about social topics. *What followed later arose in the context of entirely voluntary and personal choices by those present to engage in a heavy early hours drinking session.*

The judge held:

In my judgement there was insufficient connection between the position in which Mr Major was employed and the assault to make it right for the defendant to be held liable under the principle of social justice which goes back to the time of Holt CJ.

This decision was reversed by the Court of Appeal on 11 October 2018. It turned to *Mohamud* and Lord Toulson's analysis to answer two questions:-

(i) What was the nature of the Managing Director Mr Majors job? This question was to be answered broadly, Lady Justice Asplin noted, and it was clear from the judge's findings of fact that:

Mr Major was the directing mind and will of NR, had a wide remit and was in overall charge of all aspects of NR's business…he would have viewed the maintenance of his managerial authority as a central part of his role and that NR had a "round-the clock" business, such that there was always an employee on call.

(ii) Given the context, the place and the circumstances was Mr Major acting with the field of his activities assigned to him as managing director of NR when the assault took place or was he present in the lobby merely as a fellow reveller? Was he acting within the field of activities assigned to him by NR when he lectured a group of people including NR employees at 3am in the morning in a hotel lobby when both he and they were seriously inebriated and when he then went on to assault Mr Bellman?

When answering the first question, the respondent urged the court to use the yardstick of actual authority when deciding whether Mr Major was a reveller or a Managing Director when he punched Mr Bellman. Lady Justice Asplin rejected this approach. *The question is "what is the nature of the job?" If one focusses on actual authority one eschews a broad approach altogether.*

When answering the second question, she referred to Lord Toulson's judgement in *Mohamud* where he clarified:

> *that the cases in which there is a sufficient connection between the position in which the person is employed and his wrongful act to make it right that his employer should be held liable under the principle of social justice, are ones in which the employee has "**used or misused the position entrusted to him in a way which injured the third party.**"* [Empahsis added.] *...Such a formulation is inconsistent with a limitation imposed by the employee's actual authority. It is more consistent with the circumstances in which the employee would be held to have ostensible authority.*

Lady Justice Asplin held;

> *Even if Mr Major had taken off his managerial hat when he first arrived at the hotel, it seems to me that he chose to don it once more and to re-engage his wide remit as managing director and to misuse his position when his managerial decisions were challenged.*

Northampton Recruitment was vicariously liable for the assault.

Lord Justice Irwin agreed with Lady Asplin with some hesitation. He emphasised how unusual the facts were and how limited the parallels to this case will be.

He agreed with the trial judge in so far as the drinking session at the hotel was separate from the firm's Christmas party.

> *What was crucial here was that the discussions about work became an exercise in laying down the law by Mr Major, indeed an explicit assertion of his authority, vehemently and crudely expressed by him, with the intention of quelling dissent. That exercise of authority was something he was entitled to carry out if he chose to do so, and whoever unwise it may have been to do so in such circumstances, it did arise from the "field of activity" assigned to him.*
>
> *It cannot of course be the test that there must be actual authority to commit the tort complained of. This case arose because of the way in which Mr Major chose to exert his authority, indeed his dominance as the only real decision-maker, in the company. Hence there is liability.*

CONCLUSION

Mohamud appears to have broadened the meaning of the phrase *in the course of employment* to *in the field of its activities.* The case confirms that the close connection test is very flexible and may fix organisations with vicarious liability contrary to what seems to be indicated by the criteria applied in earlier authorities, designed though they are to give effect to recognised policy considerations.

CHAPTER FIVE

INTENTIONAL TORTS – SEXUAL ASSAULT – STAGE TWO OF THE TWO STAGE TEST

> Are the torts *so closely connected with his employment that it would be fair and just to hold the employers vicariously liable?*
> – Lord Steyn in *Lister v Hesley Hall Limited* [2002] 1 AC 215

INTRODUCTION

Salmond's test came to be regarded as inadequate for intentional torts, especially in cases of sexual abuse of children. When the test was applied, no vicarious liability attached, although the public policy considerations pointed in the opposite direction, towards the imposition of liability on the employer. In 2002 the House of Lords solved the difficulty by formulating the close connection test.

EMPLOYEES

In *Lister v Hesley Hall Limited* [2002] 1 AC 215 the House of Lords held as a matter of legal principle that the owners and managers of a school could be vicariously liable for sexual assaults committed by an employee who was the warden of a boarding house attached to the school.

Children with emotional and behavioural difficulties were sent to the school by local authorities. The assaults occurred between

1979 and 1982. The warden had been sentenced to seven years imprisonment for multiple offences of sexual abuse in the early 1990s. The critical question was whether this conduct was carried out in the course of employment.

The trial judge considered the judgement given by Butler-Sloss LJ three years previously in *T v North Yorkshire County Council* [1999] LGR 584. She said, applying the Salmond test (see above):

> *But in the field of serious sexual misconduct, I find it difficult to visualise circumstances in which an act of a teacher can be an unauthorised mode of carrying out an authorised act, although I would not wish to close the door on the possibility.*

This decision of the Court of Appeal had to be followed and the trial judge held that Hesley Hall Limited, which owned and managed the school, was not vicariously liable for the sexual abuse carried out by its employee the warden. However, the defendant did owe the claimants a duty of care to take all reasonable steps to safeguard them in their physical, moral and educational development while at the school. In a curious twist, the judge found that the defendant was vicariously liable for the warden's failure to report the acts of abuse, in breach of his duty of care to the boys.

The defendant successfully appealed to the Court of Appeal which held:

> *The simple point in this case is that if the wrongful conduct is outside the course of employment, a failure to prevent or report that wrongful conduct cannot be within the scope of employment so as to make the employer vicariously liable for that failure when the employer was not vicariously liable for the*

> *wrongful conduct itself.* The Court of Appeal was, of course, bound by its own judgement in *T v North Yorkshire County Council.*

Before the appeal was heard by the House of Lords, the Supreme Court in Canada gave judgement in two sexual abuse cases: *Bazley v Curry* (1999) and *Jacobi v Phillips* (1999). It held that vicarious liability could attach for the sexual abuse of children by employees. Much of the reasoning was based on clearly enunciated policy considerations. However, the legal test was framed in terms of close connection, with Salmond's test containing the germ for this idea. These cases were of assistance to the House of Lords in deciding unanimously to overturn the decision in *T v North Yorkshire County Council*.

Lord Steyn confirmed the question to be answered was *whether the warden's torts were so closely connected with his employment that it would be fair and just to hold the employers vicariously liable.* In formulating this test he referred to Salmond as set out below. The emphasis is his:

> "*...a master...is liable even for acts which he has not authorised, provided they are* ***so connected*** *with acts which he has authorised, that they might rightly* ***be regarded*** *as modes – although improper modes – of doing them.*"

When applying the close connection test Lord Steyn confirmed that a broad approach was to be adopted:

> *... it is not necessary to ask the simplistic question whether in the cases under consideration the acts of sexual abuse were modes of doing authorised acts. It becomes possible to consider*

> *the question of vicarious liability on the basis that the employer undertook to care for the boys through the services of the warden and that there is a very close connection between the torts of the warden and his employment. After all, they were committed in the time and on the premises of employers while the warden was also busy caring for the children.*

Lord Millett provided helpful clarification when he said:

> *it is no answer to say that the employee was guilty of intentional wrongdoing, or that his act was not merely tortious but criminal, or that he was acting exclusively for his own benefit, or that he was acting contrary to express instructions, or that his conduct was the very negation of his employer's duty.*

He also noted that there is an inherent risk of indecent assaults by persons in a position of authority on residents in boarding schools, prisons, nursing homes, and other residential homes of the young and vulnerable, *particularly if they are in close proximity to them and occupying a position of trust.* He considered holding the school vicariously liable was in accordance with the underlying rationale for the principle. Presumably by this he meant the defendant's business enterprise had increased the risk of assaults to the claimants.

In *Maga v The Trustees of the Birmingham Archdiocese of the Roman Catholic Church* [2010] EWCA Civ 256 the defendant admitted, for the purposes of this action only, that it had employed the priest who had sexually assaulted the claimant. This meant the court only had to consider stage 2 of the test.

Lord Neuberger MR provided this description of the wrongdoer who, like the police constable in the Jamaican case, had successfully disappeared by the time of the trial (last heard of in Australia, after passing through Ireland):

> *Father Clonan was, on any view, an unusual priest. In 1972, a few months after he had been ordained, when he was thirty, he started work as one of the priests at the Church of Christ the King in Coventry ("the Church"). He was very energetic, and took on various responsibilities particularly when it came to the young. For instance, he started a disco, a social club, and other clubs for the young, and he ran a number of football teams. He decided, and obtained consent from the Archdiocese, to construct a community centre ("the centre") in the curtilage of the Church. His father owned and ran a successful building company, and Father Clonan himself ran a construction business, which carried out, or at least supervised, this, and indeed other work for the Church, and indeed, for other churches in the Archdiocese. He was relatively well off and appears to have owned at least two houses in the Coventry area. He also always had at least one sports car. He was pretty liberal with his money, especially when it came to paying boys for "odd jobs…around the Church, for cleaning his car or for brushing the snooker table" in the social club…..*

The claimant suffered from learning difficulties and was 12 or 13 years old when, in 1975 to 1976, he was abused by Father Clonan. Importantly, neither the claimant nor his family were Roman Catholics or attended the Church. In 1974 a parent had complained to Father McTernan, the priest in charge at the

Church, who also lived in the presbytery, about Father Conlan having sexually assaulted his son when he was serving as an altar boy.

The claimant met Father Clonan when he stopped to admire the priest's Triumph Stag. They got talking and Father Clonan invited him to attend the Church disco. The discos were open to all young people in the area, whether or not they were Roman Catholics, and the claimant attended on several occasions. He used to help clear up afterwards and started doing odd jobs, such as cleaning Father Clonan's car and cleaning the presbytery where Father Clonan and the two other priests attached to the Church lived. The claimant ironed Father Clonan's shirts and helped clean at least one of the houses he owned. He worked in the Church on one occasion only. He was first abused in the priest's room in the presbytery and it is likely that most of the abuse occurred there. On one occasion he was abused in one of Father Clonan's houses and on another occasion in one of his cars.

The trial judge decided the Archdiocese was not vicariously liable for the sexual abuse and dismissed the claim. Although Father Conlan's employment as a priest gave him the opportunity to abuse the claimant, he was not concerned with his evangelisation or bringing the claimant into the Church. His relationship with him was restricted to cleaning and ironing jobs, which were not priestly activities.

The Court of Appeal disagreed. Lord Neuberger noted:

> *the issue, although very much fact –dependent, is ultimately one of law rather than an inference from facts, and, at least in this case, the Judge had no particular advantage over this court by*

his having seen live witnesses. .. there are a number of factors which, when taken together, persuade me that there was a sufficiently close connection between Father Conlan's employment as a priest at the Church and the abuse which he inflicted on the claimant to render it fair and just to impose vicarious liability for the abuse on his employer, the Archdiocese.

There were seven factors which he took into account:-

1. The priest normally wore clerical garb and was so dressed when he first met the claimant at the side of his sports car. A priest has a special role of trust, responsibility and moral authority;

2. The evidence confirmed his duties as a priest included the duty to evangelise. He was "*obliged to befriend non Roman Catholics*" and "*to gain and be worthy of their trust*". *Accordingly he was ostensibly performing his duty as a priest employed by the Archdiocese by getting to know the claimant.*

3. Father Conlon was given special responsibility for youth work at the Church, and the claimant was only 12 to 13 years old when the association with him began. The priest *was ostensibly carrying out one of his specifically assigned functions* when getting to know the claimant.

4. The priest developed his relationship with the claimant by inviting him to a disco which was on Church premises and which he organised as priest at the Church. *Thus, the claimant was drawn in to the relationship through the medium of a Church organised function carried on in Church premises by Father Conlan, a priest at the Church.*

5. The relationship was further developed by asking the claimant to help clear up after the discos. *Thus, Father Conlan's roles a priest in the Archdiocese gave him the status and opportunity to draw the claimant further into his sexually abusive orbit by ostensibly respectable means connected to his employment as a priest at the Church.*

6. The claimant carried out cleaning and ironing in the presbytery, adjoining the Church. It was owned by the Archdiocese and the priest lived there. The judge decided this was relevant on account of items 1 – 3 above.

7. The first incident of sexual abuse, as well as a number of subsequent incidents, occurred in Father Conlon's room at the presbytery. The evidence confirmed: *the normal course of a priest's work* would involve him *spending some time alone with people who were searching for truth.* The judge explained the fact the priest was spending time alone with the claimant for illegal sexual purposes rather than evangelisation was not the point.

<u>Primary liability of employer</u>

Lord Neuberger also found that the Archdiocese owed the claimant a duty of care following the complaint to Father McTernan of Father Conlon's assault on another boy. In the seventies, the duty did not extend to alerting the police or the Church authorities. However, Father McTernan, who was in charge at the Church, should have been observant after the complaint, irrespective of any denial given by Father Conlon. Had he performed his duty he would have been aware that Father Conlon was bringing the claimant into his room on his own and would have stopped it, thus preventing the abuse which took some time to develop.

In holding there was such a duty the judge relied on the test propounded by Lord Bridge in Caparo Industries plc v Dickman [1990] 2 AC 605 which Lord Neuberger set out as follows:

> *..."in addition to the foreseeability of damage", the "relationship" between the parties must be "one of 'proximity' or 'neighbourhood' and the situation should be one in which the court considers it fair, just and reasonable that the law should impose a duty of a given scope on the one party for the benefit of the other".*

In a very helpful passage Lord Neuberger went on to explain it was easy to envisage circumstances where an employer might not be vicariously liable but might be in breach of its own duty of care in respect of sexual abuse committed by an employee:

> *A school would not normally be vicariously liable for sexual abuse committed against a pupil by a gardener employed at the school, but, if the school had received previous allegations against the gardener of sexual abuse of pupils, failure to deal appropriately with those complaints so that he committed the abuse complained of would, at least on the face of it, give rise to a claim in negligence against the school.*

Lord Justice Longmore clarified that it was not necessary to establish that an undertaking had responsibility, similar to that of a school or local authority to its children, a la *Lister*, for vicarious liability to apply. Such responsibility is but one instance in which the test of close connection enunciated by Salmond may be satisfied. Since this case was not covered by previous authority it might be necessary to look at the policy underlying vicarious liability. It was difficult to say precisely what that was. _Lister_ had not given any definitive guidance on this.

In describing the Roman Catholic Church he said;

> *Like many other religions, it has a special concern for the vulnerable and the oppressed. That concern may not be quite the same as the legal obligation to care or assumption of responsibility for care that was emphasised by Lord Steyn or Lord Hobhouse in _Lister_ but it seems to me analogous.*
>
> *In the case of the Roman Catholic Church, this situation is further emphasised by its claim to be the authoritative source of Christian values. For centuries the Church has encouraged lay persons to look up to (and indeed revere) their priests. The Church clothes them in clerical garb and bestows on them the title of Father, a title which Father Conlan was happy to use. It is difficult to think of a role nearer to that of a parent than that of a priest. In this circumstance the absence of any formal legal responsibility is almost beside the point.*

NON EMPLOYEES

In _the Christian Brothers case_ Lord Philips considered stage 2 of the test and when an act of sexual abuse might give rise to vicarious liability. He noted that it is a more difficult question in relation to sexual abuse than negligence.

He said:

> *Although the law in this area is developing, there are some priests who do not serve under contracts of employment and the question then arises whether the priest has a relationship with anybody that can give rise to vicarious liability on the part of the body. If there is such a body, the second question is whether there is a connection between the priest's relationship with that body and the sexual abuse committed by the priest that can make that body vicariously liable for the priest's action*

The judge reviewed the Canadian case of *Bazley v Curry* where tortfeasors were lay employees.

> *There must be a strong connection between what the employer was asking the employee to do (the risk created by the employer's enterprise) and the wrongful act. It must be possible to say that the employee significantly increased the risk of harm by putting the employee in his or her position and requiring him to perform the assigned tasks.*

> *Starting with the Canadian authorities a common theme can be traced through most of the cases to which I have referred. Vicarious liability is imposed where a defendant, whose relationship with the abuser put it in a position to use the abuser to carry on its business or to further its own interests, has done so in a manner which has created or significantly enhanced the risk that the victim or victims would suffer the relevant abuse. The essential closeness of connection between the relationship between the defendant and the tortfeasor and the acts of abuse thus involves a strong causative link.*

These are the criteria that establish the necessary "close connection' between relationship and abuse. I do not think that it is right to say the creation of risk is simply a policy consideration and not one of the criteria. Creation of risk is not enough, of itself, to give rise to vicarious liability for abuse but it is always likely to be an important element in the facts that give rise to such liability.

Living cloistered on the school premises were vulnerable boys. They were triply vulnerable. They were vulnerable because they were children in the school; they were vulnerable because they were virtually prisoners in the school. And they were vulnerable because their personal histories made it even less likely that they would be believed. The brother teachers were placed in the school to care for the religious and educational needs of these pupils. Abusing the boys in their care was diametrically opposed to those objectives but, paradoxically, that very fact was one of the factors that provided the necessary close connection between the abuse and the relationship between the brothers and the Institute that gives rise to vicarious liability on the part of the latter.

FROLICS

GB v Stoke City Football Club Ltd [2015] EWHC 2862

In 2015 the claimant, an apprentice footballer, claimed damages for assault known as "gloving" against a professional footballer (second defendant) employed by Stoke City Football Club (first defendant). It was alleged there were two assaults by the footballer, one when the claimant was aged sixteen, and one when aged seventeen. Both defendants denied the assaults.

The claimant maintained that gloving was accepted practice. He accepted that there was no sexual motivation and that they were best described as *intimate physical assaults.* The judge dismissed the case as the claimant had not proved to the civil standard that the assaults had occurred. Nevertheless HH Judge Butler, sitting as a High Court judge in the Preston District Registry, went on to consider vicarious liability. If the assaults had been proved he would have decided no vicarious liability attached to the football club, since the second defendant had no *formal duties or powers in relation to the apprentices... it would have been conduct of a kind analogous to that in the cases described by Longmore LJ in <u>Graham</u> as ones in which it is inappropriate to impose vicarious liability.*

In the course of giving judgement the judge referred to the Court of Appeal's decision in *<u>Mohamud</u>*, which had ruled there was no vicarious liability. This case was subsequently overturned by the Supreme Court.

<u>X v Kuoni Travel</u> [2016] EWHC 3090 arose out of the rape of the claimant by an electrician at the hotel where she was staying on a package holiday with her husband in Sri Lanka. The rape occurred after a drunken altercation with her husband during the early hours of one morning. She had packed her suitcase and was walking through the grounds to reception in order to complain about the noise emanating from a room nearby. On the way the electrician intercepted her and told her he knew a shortcut. Believing him to be a security guard employed by the hotel the claimant followed him into an engineering room where she was

sexually assaulted and raped. The claim was brought under the Package Holiday and Package Tour Regulations 1992. However, the judge also addressed the issue of vicarious liability. He held vicarious liability could not attach since the perpetrator was an electrician rather than a security guard and there was an insufficiently close connection between the assaults and his duties so as to make it just for the defendant to be held liable. *The claimant merely bumped into the employee during the night and was offered as shortcut to reception. That offer had no connection whatsoever with these duties.*

CONCLUSION

It is difficult to avoid vicarious liability for sexual assaults on children since they are so often committed while the children are in the organisation's care. This means the employer's enterprise is increasing the risk and so should be vicariously liable for injury resulting from that risk as a matter of public policy.

CHAPTER SIX
RELIANCE TORTS

> *It is well established that merely providing the opportunity for wrongdoing is not sufficient without more to give rise to vicarious liability, absent a holding out of someone … as having authority…*
>
> – Per Lord Justice Flaux in *Frederick and others v Positive Solutions (Financial Services) Limited* [2018] EWCA Civ 431.

INTRODUCTION

The principle of vicarious liability is not limited to claims for personal injury. It arguably extends to reliance torts encompassing the relationship of principle and agent and associated claims for pure economic loss. *Dubai Aluminium Company Limited v Salaam* [2002] UKHL 48 is the leading case in this category.

Reliance torts provided early cases in support of the proposition that an employer could be liable for the dishonest conduct and criminal acts of its employees, even though the behaviour had been prohibited, either expressly or by implication. In one category of case, typically involving some sort of bailment, the employer assumes responsibility to a third party and passes that responsibility on to an agent or employee. In *Morrison v CW Martin & Sons Ltd* [1966] 1WB 716 an employee stole a fur that a customer had left with the defendant for cleaning. The defendant had entrusted the fur to an employee to carry out this task when the theft occurred. It was held that the defendant was vicariously liable for the theft since it was carried out in the course of employment.

The facts of *Lloyd v Grace, Smith and Co [1912] AC 716* bore more similarity to the facts of *Dubai*. Mrs Lloyd was duped by the Managing Clerk of the defendant firm of solicitors to hand over the deeds of several cottages she owned which he transferred into his own name. The firm had held the clerk out as having authority to act on behalf of its partners. Since Mrs Lloyd acted in reliance on this authority, vicarious liability attached to the partners of the firm.

Dubai was different from Lloyd in that there was no holding out or resulting reliance by the claimant.

DUBAI ALUMINIUM

The case arose out of an elaborate fraud as a consequence of which the claimant company lost millions of dollars to a bogus consultancy company. The claimant's chief executive was one of several dishonest participants in the scheme, as was the defendant, Mr Salaam. He was a client of a firm of solicitors called Amhurst. The senior partner, Mr Amhurst himself, dealt with his affairs and had drafted the consultancy agreement signed by the chief executive of *Dubal.* Although the partner did not benefit from the fraud, apart from the firm receiving fees in payment for his work, the claimant company alleged that Mr Amhurst dishonestly assisted in the fraud. The company sued him and also his firm which it said was vicariously liable for his fraudulent activities. It was common ground that Mr Amhurst's partners were innocent of any fraudulent activity.

At various stages of the trial all the defendants settled with the claimant by agreeing to pay large amounts. The claims against Mr Amhurst and the Amhurst firm were settled by the firm for $10 million. That left contribution claims brought by some of the defendants against each other and against third parties. The Amhurst firm received a complete indemnity from two of the fraudsters, including its client Mr Salaam. Both individuals appealed to the Court of Appeal which allowed the appeal. It held that the Amhurst firm was not vicariously liable for the acts of its senior partner so there was no basis on which it could claim contribution from Salaam and the other fraudster. The Amhurst firm appealed to the House of Lords.

In the words of Lord Nicholls of Birkenhead:-

> *The contribution claim made by the Amhurst firm in respect of its payment of $10 million to Dubai Aluminium is based on the Civil Liability (Contribution) Act 1978. Section 1 (1) of this Act (the "Contribution Act") provides that any person " liable" in respect of any damage suffered by another person may recover contribution from any other person liable in respect of the same damage. On the judge's findings Mr Salaam and Mr Al Jajir were liable in respect of Dubai Aluminium's loss. That is clear. In order to found a contribution claim the Amhurst firm had to show it, too, was "liable" in respect of the loss suffered by Dubai Aluminium. The Amhurst firm claimed it satisfied this prerequisite because, pursuant to section 10 of the*

> *Partnership Act 1890, it was liable for Mr Amhurst's alleged wrongdoing. Thus, so it claimed, the case falls squarely within the scope of section 1 (1) of the Contribution Act.*

Section 10 of the Partnership Act 1890 provides:-

> *Where, by any wrongful act or omission of any partner acting in the ordinary course of the business of the firm, or with the authority of his co-partners, loss or injury is caused to any person not being a partner in the firm, or any penalty is incurred, the firm is liable therefor to the same extent as the partner so acting or omitting to act.*

The fraudsters alleged that the Amhurst firm was not vicariously liable on two grounds:-

1. The cause of action asserted by Dubai Aluminium against Mr Amhurst, which was the equitable wrong of breach of fiduciary duty, did not fall within the meaning of section 10. The House of Lords disagreed. The section is not limited to tortious wrongdoing.

2. Alternatively, the acts were not carried out by Mr Amhurst in the ordinary course of the business of the firm. He had drafted the consultancy agreement with Dubai Aluminium . This was said to have provided dishonest assistance to the chief executive of the claimant to act in breach of its fiduciary duties.

After noting that the absence of authority is not the *touchstone* for deciding vicarious liability, otherwise the policy considerations that underlie the principle would be undermined, Lord Nicholls had the following to say about the close connection test:-

> *This "close connection' test focuses attention in the right direction. But it affords no guidance on the type or degree of connection which will normally be regarded as sufficiently close to prompt the legal conclusion that the risk of the wrongful act occurring, and any loss flowing from the wrongful act, should fall on the firm or employer rather than the third party who was wronged. ... Again, the well-known dictum of Lord Dunedin in Plumb v Cobden Flour Mills Co Ltd [1914] AC 62 draws a distinction between prohibitions which limit the sphere of employment and those which only deal with conduct within the sphere of employment. This leaves open how to recognise one from the other.*
>
> *This lack of precision is inevitable, given the infinite range of circumstances where the issue arises. The crucial feature or features, either producing or negativing vicarious liability, vary widely from one case or type of case to the next. Essentially the court makes an evaluative judgement in each case, having regard to all the circumstances and, importantly, having regard also to the assistance provided by previous court decisions. In this field the latter form of assistances is particularly valuable.*

Lord Nicholls considered a distinction was to be drawn between acts of dishonesty done for the purposes of the business and those acts carried out for the purpose of furthering the agent's or employee's own interests. In the latter case the wrongdoer was on a *frolic of his own for which no vicarious liability would attach.* This proposition has been undermined in later cases. The fact the employee or agent was acting for its own benefit does not necessarily mean he was on a frolic. It is simply one of the criteria to consider when making an assessment.

> *Drafting agreements of this nature for a proper purpose would be within the ordinary course of the firm's business. Drafting these particular agreements is to be regarded as an act done within the ordinary course of the firm's business even though they were drafted for a dishonest purpose. These acts were so closely connected with the acts Mr Amhurst was authorised to do that for the purpose of the liability of the Amhurst firm they may fairly and properly be regarded as done by him while acting in the ordinary course of the firm's business.*

On apportionment of liability between the dishonesty or negligence of an employee or agent and the employer or principal who is vicariously liable Lord Hobhouse asked whether it was *just and equitable to distinguish between the actual fault of the former and the vicarious liability of the latter?*

> *As between the servant and his employer (or agent and his principal), clearly it is prima facie just and equitable to make a distinction. But it will not necessarily be as simple as that. The relationship between them will normally be contractual and include express terms or implied terms to the benefit of one or other party which have a decisive impact. For instance, there may be terms concerning the provision of insurance cover. The apportionment, as between them, will have to take such factors into account.*

Lord Millett seized on the question and answered it in a succinct and logical way, which prefigured the reasoning in Viasystems (see chapter two). Since the vicariously liable employer is substituted for the wrongdoer, the innocence of the employer is irrelevant. Where both the employer and the wrongdoer are joined, liability is apportioned between them equally or 50/50 for the damage the wrongdoer has caused.

LIABILITY ESTABLISHED

Khaskshouri v Jimenez and Cash [2017] EWHC 3392 is a recent case in the High Court that concerned a claim for damages in deceit. A London football club was in dire financial difficulties when a director and majority shareholder persuaded a personal friend, the claimant Mr Khaskshouri, to make a short-term loan of £1.8 million in order to ward off administration. He agreed to make the loan in return for a share in a Land Deal concerning the Club stadium when the Club was sold. So as to free up capital in order to make the loan, the claimant sold part of his interest in a lucrative property development scheme in Los Angeles.

The judge found that he was induced to make the loan by the following misrepresentations from his old friend Mr Jimenez, the first defendant, on his own behalf and on behalf of the second Defendant director Kevin Cash, also an old friend:-

1. Tony Jimenez and Kevin Cash were the majority shareholders and controllers of the club;

2. In their capacity as such they would make sure that the Club was not sold without a Land Deal being in place. If Mr Khakshouri advanced the loan he would be given a 30% interest in the Defendants' share of the Land Deal.

After the claimant had made the loan, potential purchasers of the club melted away. Eventually a buyer was found who wanted to do a quick deal. He persuaded the directors to sell the club without any Land Deal.

The judge found that the first defendant made the representations knowing that they were untrue and to induce the claimant to make the loan. He was liable in deceit and the second defendant was vicariously liable for the deceit.

The claimant had argued that the second defendant had given the first defendant actual authority to negotiate the loan on his behalf. The second defendant left it to the first defendant to agree the terms of the Land Deal and also authorised the first defendant to offer a percentage which would inevitably reduce his own interest in the Land Deal. This was denied. The second defendant maintained the first defendant was acting on behalf of the club, rather than on his own behalf. However the second defendant had signed a Side Letter confirming that he had given the first defendant express authority to deal with the claimant. The judge found:

> *The representations made by Mr Jimenez were squarely within the authority conferred by Mr Cash. They were necessary to persuade* [the claimant] *to enter into the Loan which kept the Club afloat and enabled him and Mr Jimenez to pursue the Land Deal which was for their persona benefits.*

The judge decided that the second defendant had authorised the first defendant to negotiate a land deal with the Claimant and this authorisation included all the representations the first defendant had made. Accordingly, the second defendant was vicariously liable for the deceit of the first defendant.

LIABILITY AVOIDED

A more recent case is *Frederick and others v Positive Solutions (Financial Services) Limited* [2018] EWCA Civ 431.

The claimants were a family. One of them was approached by an old schoolfriend, Mr Qureshi, who persuaded them to make short term loans in a property development scheme that his business partner, Luke Warren, was intending to carry out in Wembley. At the end of six months they would secure a fixed return on their investment and the return of the monies.

Mr Quereshi explained that the family could raise the money needed by re-mortgaging various properties they owned. Luke Warren could arrange this as an Independent Financial Adviser employed or authorised by the defendant. It was accepted that none of the family ever met or had any dealings with Luke Warren or the defendant. The defendant operated through agents of which Luke Warren was one.

Luke Warren submitted the mortgage applications through an online portal operated by Abbey National to which he had access as a representative of the defendant. The information he submitted was false to justify the borrowing and obtain the money. Some of the money released was advanced by the claimants to

Luke Warren and a company of which he and Mr Qureshi were directors. The money was misappropriated and lost in the property development and Mr Warren went bankrupt. The claimants were left with mortgages on their properties which they could not discharge.

They sued the defendant and alleged it was vicariously liable for Luke Warren. The defendant responded with an application for summary judgement, the principle of vicarious liability was inapplicable and it could not be liable.

In entering summary judgement for the defendant, the judge decided Mr Warren had designed the fraud himself.

> *This is not a legitimate transaction that had been brought to the defendant and which the defendant had allocated to Mr Warren to undertake and which Mr Warren had undertaken in a fraudulent way.*

On appeal, Flaux LJ confirmed the Judge was right to enter summary judgement against the claimants on the issue of vicarious liability for a number of reasons. Firstly, even assuming the claimants' favour that a case of agency such as the present case was to be analysed pursuant to a unitary modern law of vicarious liability applicable in all cases, as set out in the judgement of Lord Phillips PSC in *the Christian Brothers case* as it was interpreted and summarised by Lord Reed in *Cox*, the Judge rightly concluded that the appellants could not satisfy the two stage test.

He said:

> *The reality is that, on the appellants' pleaded case, Warren was essentially engaged on a "recognisably independent business" of his and Qureshi's, the property investment scheme in which Qureshi induced the appellants' to invest. Warren then made the admittedly dishonest applications to Abbey National for re-mortgages in order to generate the funds for such investment. Warren's use of the portal was simply the means by which he was able to obtain funds from the appellants to invest in the scheme. To describe that activity as in any sense an integral part of the business activities of the respondent would be a complete distortion of the true position on the facts.*

Moreover, not all the acts and omissions necessary to establish the tort of deceit took place within the alleged course of Luke Warren's employment or agency. This inevitably meant the defendant was not vicariously liable for his wrongdoing.

Lord Justice Flaux also noted that:

> *It is well established that merely providing the opportunity for wrongdoing is not sufficient without more to give rise to vicarious liability, absent a holding out of someone in Warren's position as having authority to act for the defendant sought to be made vicariously liable...There is no suggestion in the decisions of the Supreme Court in the Christian Brothers Case, Cox or Mohamud that those statements of principle do not still represent good law.*

The judge did not go further and determine whether reliance based torts committed by an agent are in a distinct category so that the principal cannot be vicariously liable unless the agent had actual or ostensible authority. Lord Reed had made it clear that agency was not being considered in *Cox.*

CONCLUSION

The two stage test for vicarious liability first set out in *the Christian Brothers case* in 2012 may not apply to cases involving reliance torts and agency. That has yet to be decided.

MORE BOOKS BY LAW BRIEF PUBLISHING

A selection of our other titles available now:-

'A Practical Guide to Immigration Law and Tier 1 Entrepreneur Applications' by Sarah Pinder
'A Practical Guide to Unlawful Eviction and Harassment' by Stephanie Lovegrove
'In My Backyard! A Practical Guide to Neighbourhood Plans' by Dr Sue Chadwick
'A Practical Guide to the Law Relating to Food' by Ian Thomas
'A Practical Guide to the Ending of Assured Shorthold Tenancies' by Elizabeth Dwomoh
'Commercial Mediation – A Practical Guide' by Nick Carr
'A Practical Guide to Financial Services Claims' by Chris Hegarty
'The Law of Houses in Multiple Occupation: A Practical Guide to HMO Proceedings' by Julian Hunt
'A Practical Guide to Unlawful Eviction and Harassment' by Stephanie Lovegrove
'A Practical Guide to Solicitor and Client Costs' by Robin Dunne
'Artificial Intelligence – The Practical Legal Issues' by John Buyers
'A Practical Guide to Wrongful Conception, Wrongful Birth and Wrongful Life Claims' by Rebecca Greenstreet
'Occupiers, Highways and Defective Premises Claims: A Practical Guide Post-Jackson – 2nd Edition' by Andrew Mckie
'A Practical Guide to Financial Ombudsman Service Claims' by Adam Temple & Robert Scrivenor
'A Practical Guide to the Law of Enfranchisement and Lease Extension' by Paul Sams
'A Practical Guide to Marketing for Lawyers – 2nd Edition' by Catherine Bailey & Jennet Ingram
'A Practical Guide to Advising Schools on Employment Law' by Jonathan Holden

'Certificates of Lawful Use and Development: A Guide to Making and Determining Applications' by Bob Mc Geady & Meyric Lewis

'A Practical Guide to the Law of Dilapidations' by Mark Shelton

'A Practical Guide to the 2018 Jackson Personal Injury and Costs Reforms' by Andrew Mckie

'A Guide to Consent in Clinical Negligence Post-Montgomery' by Lauren Sutherland QC

'A Practical Guide to Running Housing Disrepair and Cavity Wall Claims: 2nd Edition' by Andrew Mckie & Ian Skeate

'A Practical Guide to the General Data Protection Regulation (GDPR)' by Keith Markham

'A Practical Guide to Digital and Social Media Law for Lawyers' by Sherree Westell

'A Practical Guide to Holiday Sickness Claims – 2nd Edition' by Andrew Mckie & Ian Skeate

'A Practical Guide to Inheritance Act Claims by Adult Children Post-Ilott v Blue Cross' by Sheila Hamilton Macdonald

'A Practical Guide to Elderly Law' by Justin Patten

'Arguments and Tactics for Personal Injury and Clinical Negligence Claims' by Dorian Williams

'A Practical Guide to QOCS and Fundamental Dishonesty' by James Bentley

'A Practical Guide to Drone Law' by Rufus Ballaster, Andrew Firman, Eleanor Clot

'Practical Mediation: A Guide for Mediators, Advocates, Advisers, Lawyers, and Students in Civil, Commercial, Business, Property, Workplace, and Employment Cases' by Jonathan Dingle with John Sephton

'Practical Horse Law: A Guide for Owners and Riders' by Brenda Gilligan

'A Comparative Guide to Standard Form Construction and Engineering Contracts' by Jon Close

'A Practical Guide to Compliance for Personal Injury Firms Working With Claims Management Companies' by Paul Bennett

'A Practical Guide to the Landlord and Tenant Act 1954: Commercial Tenancies' by Richard Hayes & David Sawtell

'A Practical Guide to Personal Injury Claims Involving Animals' by Jonathan Hand

'A Practical Guide to Psychiatric Claims in Personal Injury' by Liam Ryan
'Introduction to the Law of Community Care in England and Wales' by Alan Robinson
'A Practical Guide to Dog Law for Owners and Others' by Andrea Pitt
'Ellis and Kevan on Credit Hire – 5th Edition' by Aidan Ellis & Tim Kevan
'RTA Allegations of Fraud in a Post-Jackson Era: The Handbook – 2nd Edition' by Andrew Mckie
'RTA Personal Injury Claims: A Practical Guide Post-Jackson' by Andrew Mckie
'On Experts: CPR35 for Lawyers and Experts' by David Boyle
'An Introduction to Personal Injury Law' by David Boyle
'A Practical Guide to Claims Arising From Accidents Abroad and Travel Claims' by Andrew Mckie & Ian Skeate
'A Practical Guide to Cosmetic Surgery Claims' by Dr Victoria Handley
'A Practical Guide to Chronic Pain Claims' by Pankaj Madan
'A Practical Guide to Claims Arising from Fatal Accidents' by James Patience
'A Practical Approach to Clinical Negligence Post-Jackson' by Geoffrey Simpson-Scott
'A Practical Guide to Personal Injury Trusts' by Alan Robinson
'Employers' Liability Claims: A Practical Guide Post-Jackson' by Andrew Mckie
'A Practical Guide to Subtle Brain Injury Claims' by Pankaj Madan
'The Law of Driverless Cars: An Introduction' by Alex Glassbrook
'A Practical Guide to Costs in Personal Injury Cases' by Matthew Hoe
'A Practical Guide to Alternative Dispute Resolution in Personal Injury Claims – Getting the Most Out of ADR Post-Jackson' by Peter Causton, Nichola Evans, James Arrowsmith
'A Practical Guide to Personal Injuries in Sport' by Adam Walker & Patricia Leonard
'The No Nonsense Solicitors' Practice: A Guide To Running Your Firm' by Bettina Brueggemann
'Baby Steps: A Guide to Maternity Leave and Maternity Pay' by Leah Waller

'The Queen's Counsel Lawyer's Omnibus: 20 Years of Cartoons from The Times 1993-2013' by Alex Steuart Williams

www.ingramcontent.com/pod-product-compliance
Lightning Source LLC
LaVergne TN
LVHW022303200926
848481LV00004B/1200